ANALYTICS AND BIG DATA
FOR ACCOUNTANTS

BY JIM LINDELL, MBA, CPA, CGMA

Notice to Readers

Analytics and Big Data for Accountants is intended solely for use in continuing professional education and not as a reference. It does not represent an official position of the Association of International Certified Professional Accountants, and it is distributed with the understanding that the author and publisher are not rendering legal, accounting, or other professional services in the publication. This course is intended to be an overview of the topics discussed within, and the author has made every attempt to verify the completeness and accuracy of the information herein. However, neither the author nor publisher can guarantee the applicability of the information found herein. If legal advice or other expert assistance is required, the services of a competent professional should be sought.

> **You can qualify to earn free CPE through our pilot testing program.**
> **If interested, please visit aicpa.org at http://apps.aicpa.org/secure/CPESurvey.aspx.**

Course Code: **746272**
DAAN GS-0417-0A
Revised: **April 2017**

TABLE OF CONTENTS

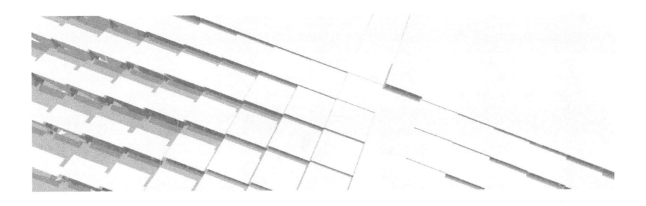

OVERVIEW

WELCOME TO ANALYTICS AND BIG DATA FOR ACCOUNTANTS!

Analytics is a new force driving business. Tools have been created to measure program effects and return on investment, visualize data and business processes, and uncover the relationship between key performance indicators—many using the unprecedented amount of data now moving into organizations. In this course, you will discuss leading-edge topics in analytics and finance in a session that is packed with useful tips and practical guidance that you can apply immediately.

INTRODUCTORY COMMENTS

One of the first times the author was exposed to the concept of Big Data was when he served as the CFO for a large non-profit early in his career. The organization was going through a major organization restructure, and it was also restructuring its information technology infrastructure and the software tools used to provide information technology services. As a result, the agency brought in an expert on a fourth-generation language database program. The expert had a wife who was suffering from a severe illness. The expert was adamant that if he could obtain a large number of patient records, he would find a cure for his wife's illness. His contention was that a relationship between the illness and the cure was hidden within other patient records. He certainly had the skills to find a connection. The author saw the concept of Big Data first-hand without realizing how it would evolve. The author is more convinced than ever that the accountant position is morphing daily. Transaction analysis, variance analysis, and ratio analysis are all being performed by software packages. The accountant role will continue its migration from data creator, manipulator, and archivist to one of data scientist and storyteller. It is imperative that the accountant of today keep pace with technological change and recognize the need to move from historical analysis to predictive change and ultimately, prescriptive change.

It's against this backdrop that the advent of Big Data and analytics has already affected many organizations and will play a much more significant role in the future.

TOPICS DISCUSSED

- Evidence-based techniques for finding or generating data, selecting key performance indicators, isolating program effects
- Relating data to return on investment, financial values, and executive decision-making
- Data sources including surveys, interviews, customer satisfaction, engagement, and operational data
- Visualizing and presenting complex results

THE CHAPTERS IN THIS COURSE

- Chapter 1: What Are Big Data and Analytics?
- Chapter 2: Big Data History—Big Data Sources and Characteristics
- Chapter 3: What Are the Trends in Big Data?
- Chapter 4: What Are the Strategy and Business Applications of Big Data?
- Chapter 5: Big Data Platforms and Operating Tools
- Chapter 6: Big Data End User and Accounting Tools
- Chapter 7: Examples of Big Data
- Chapter 8: Big Data in the Accounting Department
- Chapter 9: Ethics and Privacy With Big Data

OPENING DISCUSSION

As you progress through the course, consider the following challenges:

- What information does your organization currently have access to that is already in your systems and available for use?
- What information could you have access to that exists in your organization but is not captured?
- What information exists on the Internet in regards to industry databases or government databases that you could access?
- What information is available through sensors and machines that could provide insights into the operational and strategic dynamics of your business?

EXERCISE

It would be helpful to spend a couple of minutes to jot down the type of information your organization currently has available. This analysis will be helpful as you consider different applications of analytics and Big Data. Use table 0-1 to gather your information.

Table 0-1 What Information Does Your Organization Have Available?

	Customer	Vendor	Employee	Strategic	Operational	Other
What Information Do You Have?						
1	1	1	1	1	1	
2	2	2	2	2	2	
3	3	3	3	3	3	
4	4	4	4	4	4	
5	5	5	5	5	5	
6	6	6	6	6	6	
7	7	7	7	7	7	
8	8	8	8	8	8	
9	9	9	9	9	9	
10	10	10	10	10	10	

Before becoming immersed in the overall topic, it may be useful to discuss a broad picture of Big Data so that all participants have an initial understanding. Consider illustration 0-1:

Illustration 0-1

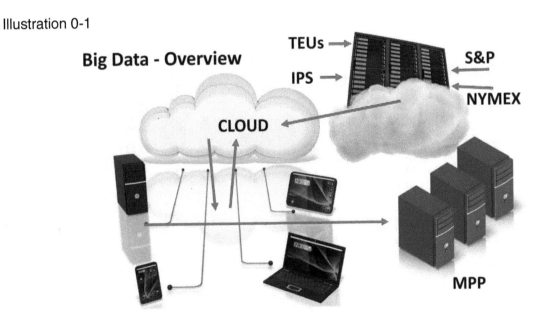

TEUs—Twenty-Foot Equivalent Units

IPS—Industrial Production Statistics

S&P—Standard & Poor's

NYMEX—New York Mercantile Exchange

MPP—Massively Parallel Processing

Data originates in a variety of places and in a variety of forms. Data from individual companies, organizations, streaming data, and so on accumulate in the cloud, as shown in illustration 0-1. Organizations access the information via in-house servers, laptops, tablets and other mobile devices. Organizations may desire a unique combination of external databases and internal databases, including calculations, projections, and so on. That information is sent to multiple computers with individual processors to analyze the vast amounts of data. These multiple computers with their processors are known as massively parallel processing (MPP).

EXAMPLE

Next, we will consider a simple example of how large amounts of data can be processed to help you create a narrative to supplement your accounting processes. Let us assume that our company is in the lumber industry or is affected by lumber prices. The industrial production statistics are available at www.federalreserve.gov/ RELEASES/ g17/ ipdisk/ alltables.txt. The Federal Reserve's monthly index of industrial production rates covers manufacturing, mining, and electric and gas utilities. The production index measures real output and is expressed as a percentage of real output.

The initial data found on that website looks like that in table 0-2. This raw data is overwhelming and not easy to interpret in its current form.

Table 0-2

```
"B50001: Total index"
"IPS.B50001"   1919    5.0354   4.8128   4.6737   4.7572   4.7850   5.0910   5.3970   5.4805   5.3692   5.3136   5.2301   5.3136
"IPS.B50001"   1920    5.8143   5.8143   5.7030   5.3970   5.5361   5.5918   5.4527   5.4805   5.2857   5.0632   4.6459   4.3677
"IPS.B50001"   1921    4.1173   4.0339   3.9226   3.9226   4.0339   4.0060   3.9782   4.1173   4.1451   4.3955   4.3399   4.3121
"IPS.B50001"   1922    4.4790   4.6737   4.9241   4.7572   5.0075   5.2579   5.1466   5.4248   5.4248   5.7309   5.9812   6.1482
"IPS.B50001"   1923    6.0091   6.0925   6.2873   6.4263   6.5098   6.4542   6.3985   6.2873   6.1481   6.1203   6.1203   5.9812
"IPS.B50001"   1924    6.1203   6.2316   6.1203   5.9256   5.6752   5.4248   5.3414   5.5361   5.7309   5.8700   5.9812   6.1482
"IPS.B50001"   1925    6.3429   6.3429   6.3429   6.3985   6.3707   6.3151   6.4820   6.3707   6.2873   6.5376   6.6767   6.7602
"IPS.B50001"   1926    6.6489   6.6489   6.7324   6.7324   6.6767   6.7602   6.7880   6.8715   6.9827   6.9827   6.9549   6.9271
"IPS.B50001"   1927    6.8993   6.9549   7.0384   6.8715   6.9271   6.8993   7.0384   7.1775   7.2331   7.3722   7.5113   7.6504
"IPS.B50001"   1928    6.7324   6.7880   6.8436   6.8158   6.8993   6.9549   7.0384   7.1775   7.2331   7.3722   7.5113   7.6504
"IPS.B50001"   1929    7.7617   7.7339   7.7617   7.9008   8.0399   8.0955   8.2068   8.1234   8.0677   7.9286   7.5391   7.2053
"IPS.B50001"   1930    7.2053   7.1775   7.0662   7.0106   6.8993   6.7045   6.3985   6.2594   6.1482   5.9812   5.8421   5.7030
"IPS.B50001"   1931    5.6752   5.7030   5.8143   5.8421   5.7587   5.6196   5.5361   5.3414   5.0910   4.8963   4.8406   4.8128
"IPS.B50001"   1932    4.6737   4.5624   4.5068   4.2008   4.0617   3.9226   3.8113   3.9226   4.1730   4.3121   4.3121   4.2286
"IPS.B50001"   1933    4.1451   4.1730   3.9226   4.2008   4.8963   5.6474   6.1760   5.9256   5.5918   5.3136   5.0075   5.0354
"IPS.B50001"   1934    5.2023   5.4527   5.7030   5.7030   5.8143   5.7030   5.3136   5.2579   4.9519   5.1745   5.2301   5.5639
"IPS.B50001"   1935    6.0091   6.1203   6.0925   5.9812   5.9812   6.0647   6.0647   6.2872   6.4489   6.6489   6.7880   6.8715
"IPS.B50001"   1936    6.7602   6.5933   6.6767   7.0940   7.2331   7.3722   7.5113   7.6226   7.7617   7.8730   8.0955   8.3459
"IPS.B50001"   1937    8.3181   8.4294   8.6241   8.6241   8.6519   8.5406   8.5963   8.5406   8.2624   7.6504   6.8993   6.2872
"IPS.B50001"   1938    6.1481   6.0925   6.0925   5.9812   5.8421   5.8978   6.2316   6.5654   6.7602   6.9271   7.2053   7.2888
"IPS.B50001"   1939    7.2888   7.3444   7.3722   7.3444   7.3166   7.4835   7.7061   7.8173   8.2903   8.7076   8.9301   8.9301
"IPS.B50001"   1940    8.8188   8.5406   8.3459   8.5128   8.7632   9.0414   9.1527   9.2083   9.4031   9.5421   9.7647   10.0985
```

I selected the IPS data for the NAICS codes B500001(Total Index Statistics for all industrial production) and G321(Wood Products Industry Statistics) to begin the analysis, as in table 0-3:

Table 0-3

IPS.B50001	2000	94.7615	95.0664	95.4649	96.1873	96.3963	96.488	96.386	96.0455	96.4354	96.1096	96.1276	95.8441
IPS.B50001	2001	95.1747	94.5581	94.2954	94.0294	93.3526	92.7435	92.249	92.05	91.7355	91.3042	90.8141	90.8243
IPS.B50001	2002	91.403	91.402	92.1252	92.5335	92.9145	93.8071	93.5978	93.6123	93.7211	93.4327	93.9229	93.4505
IPS.B50001	2003	94.0868	94.3655	94.1543	93.444	93.4875	93.5856	94.0002	93.8015	94.3862	94.4645	95.2175	95.1269
IPS.B50001	2004	95.3012	95.8359	95.3155	95.6825	96.4212	95.6445	96.3852	96.445	96.5044	97.4167	97.6225	98.3132
IPS.B50001	2005	98.7886	99.4359	99.3247	99.4595	99.6415	100.0262	99.7447	99.9372	98.0478	99.3189	100.2981	100.8948
IPS.B50001	2006	101.0256	100.9981	101.2658	101.6644	101.5254	101.9173	101.8981	102.252	102.1093	102.0843	101.9683	102.9751
IPS.B50001	2007	102.4954	103.6101	103.7575	104.5126	104.564	104.5525	104.5442	104.7213	105.0936	104.537	105.1581	105.1322
IPS.B50001	2008	104.8595	104.5926	104.2989	103.53	103.0519	102.8476	102.3093	100.7832	96.4822	97.3647	96.1487	93.3954
IPS.B50001	2009	91.2227	90.6371	89.2352	88.4857	87.5811	87.214	88.1641	89.119	89.7943	90.1731	90.4311	90.7512
IPS.B50001	2010	91.8162	92.0991	92.7191	93.0609	94.4844	94.6828	95.1542	95.4866	95.715	95.4803	95.518	96.3941
IPS.B50001	2011	96.3665	95.8776	96.6955	96.2901	96.5438	96.7612	97.1711	97.7699	97.7762	98.4296	98.2829	98.7841
IPS.B50001	2012	99.5096	99.7389	99.0887	99.928	100.0508	99.9691	100.2736	99.833	99.9189	100.1878	100.6435	100.858
IPS.B50001	2013	100.933	101.3425	101.561	101.5385	101.4689	101.6621	101.2685	102.0442	102.6361	102.6534	102.9163	103.1889
IPS.B50001	2014	103.0047	103.8079	104.6615	104.8595	105.2461	105.716	106.0803	106.1138	106.6776	106.8463	107.7996	107.9108
IPS.B50001	2015	107.6003	107.4368	107.2374	107.0599	106.6799	106.6628	107.4746	107.4973	107.5331	107.4001	106.5811	105.8689
IPS.B50001	2016	106.8477											
IPS.G321	2000	143.972	143.4722	143.9109	143.2324	140.9417	138.436	137.5802	135.2912	136.5014	133.6298	133.283	129.321
IPS.G321	2001	126.5031	125.8307	128.3142	128.6762	129.9331	130.9957	129.5036	131.7801	132.8763	129.2955	130.1209	131.9857
IPS.G321	2002	133.3057	132.8523	135.8989	135.6197	135.6325	137.4395	135.6227	136.501	135.7389	135.9186	134.1315	133.5371
IPS.G321	2003	134.3941	134.3887	132.4979	132.858	132.6237	133.6178	134.9538	134.4597	135.2376	136.3176	140.5582	137.6886
IPS.G321	2004	137.9976	138.0842	136.9454	138.3816	138.9288	136.5499	138.691	138.9603	136.4546	140.4624	140.2499	139.8354
IPS.G321	2005	146.1386	142.86	142.2799	142.6249	143.0869	143.4326	144.3807	144.0517	149.3065	156.8229	158.6932	158.6398
IPS.G321	2006	158.764	155.9862	155.0613	152.576	151.3601	149.1037	149.5498	147.233	145.8068	139.3438	138.9545	142.9898
IPS.G321	2007	140.0055	139.8647	141.9422	139.9414	141.1664	142.9497	142.5319	139.8908	138.6741	135.9987	133.9249	134.3439
IPS.G321	2008	131.3716	128.5247	127.1709	124.6709	123.2955	122.3217	121.8669	119.398	115.8094	109.9483	106.6985	96.6497
IPS.G321	2009	93.6668	93.3626	89.9492	88.3143	87.4935	90.724	90.5585	92.0024	92.1858	90.6401	91.2439	90.7279
IPS.G321	2010	92.6534	91.2404	92.4849	96.417	97.872	95.2164	94.6381	93.8519	92.8365	93.9712	94.0948	94.4015
IPS.G321	2011	94.1239	93.5283	95.8471	93.7046	94.7942	93.4226	93.6132	92.5363	94.9918	94.7417	94.766	95.8602
IPS.G321	2012	98.0903	97.4725	98.2069	99.7776	101.1851	99.1884	99.5748	99.8404	98.921	100.6659	103.2503	103.8267
IPS.G321	2013	104.9279	106.5673	105.4279	103.602	104.0396	103.9955	104.0478	105.6103	107.0795	107.7638	109.0048	107.3474
IPS.G321	2014	105.0321	104.9346	107.1353	107.6058	109.3083	109.5686	111.385	112.1464	111.1789	112.4458	112.0506	113.368
IPS.G321	2015	111.1515	110.2591	109.7365	109.574	108.836	108.8611	111.2143	111.6601	112.5653	113.3287	112.8498	114.869
IPS.G321	2016	116.2468											

Next, the monthly data was obtained for Louisiana-Pacific Corporation (LPX) from Finance.Yahoo.com, and then all three data series were combined utilizing Excel. Once the data series had been established, the graph in illustration 0-2 was generated.

Illustration 0-2

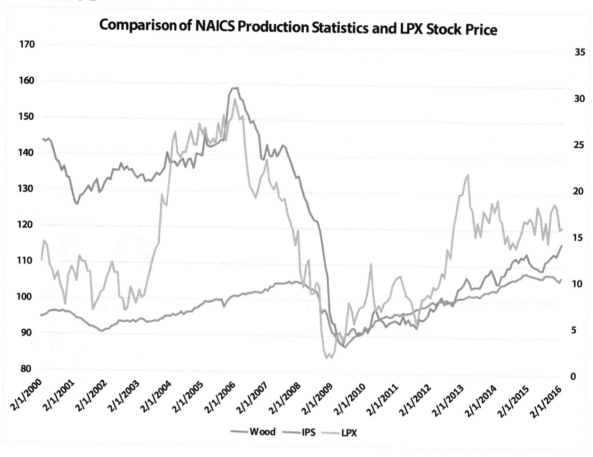

It's easy to see that in graph form, this data comes to life in a new way. As we supplement our accounting skills with storytelling and data science, is it possible to make some summary conclusions from the data in this example? My interpretation is that:

1. The wood product production statistics seem to follow along a similar trend line as the LPX stock price.
2. The major IPS also appears to follow a similar trend.
3. A supposition could be that a decline in wood production precedes an overall economic decline (note the steep decline which corresponds to the Great Recession.)
4. A supposition could be that wood production statistics during the housing bubble were supported by an increase in LPX stock prices.

By manipulating the data available in just this small example, we were able to uncover trends that could be used to make business predictions. However, most real-life examples of Big Data are much more complex than this. Most use much larger databases and more sophisticated technological tools than Excel. This example was meant to demonstrate the fundamental concept of Big Data so that you can see how powerful it is and help you relate to it.

As the course develops, we will be exploring significantly larger and more varied types of data. The software programs used to interpret Big Data are more complex than Excel, although Microsoft has created a product—Excel BI, which will most likely be the tool that accountants will prefer because of most accountants' current levels of familiarity with Excel.

By the end of this course, you should be familiar with the sources, types, and trends of Big Data as well as the various tools available for processing and interpreting this information. We'll take a look at some more examples and learn how you can apply these techniques in your own practice. Are you ready to get started?

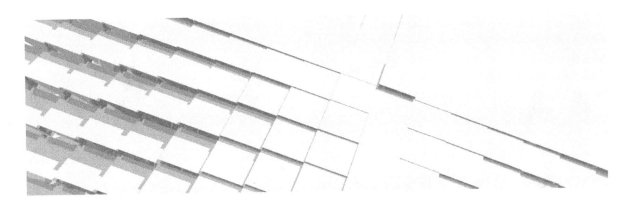

Chapter 1

WHAT ARE
BIG DATA AND ANALYTICS?

LEARNING OBJECTIVES

After completing this chapter, you should be able to do the following:

- Identify the three different types of data.
- Recall what type of data volume Big Data represents.
- Recognize Big Data terminology.

INTRODUCTION

In the early 20th century, businesses kept track of financial and operational results using paper and ink. It was difficult enough just to record the date of the transactions, let alone summarize information with financial statements. The main form of automation that helped improve the efficiency of accounting clerks was limited to innovations in carbon copy paper, mimeograph machines, copy machines, and the like. When computers finally were available for operational and financial use, the systems were based on a batch recording of transactions. Again the focus was on capturing internal data to help an organization understand its financial and operational results. As computers advanced and became more powerful, the focus increased in obtaining more internally generated operational and financial information as well as analyzing the myriad information as a result of increased computing power, increased data, and more user-friendly tools.

Prior to the advent of the Internet, an organization worked mainly with its internal data. With the subsequent advances in Internet use in the latter half of the 20th century and the beginning of the 21st century, external information became accessible that could be integrated with internal data. Companies moved from producing batch information to employees generating information (on both the corporate and personal level), to sensors producing data about all aspects of our lives. This last point can be frightening because appliances, sensors, and different apparatuses are generating more data in shorter periods of time than ever before. This has resulted in a flood of information, the concept of *Big Data*, and predictive analytics.

DEFINITION—WHAT IS BIG DATA?

What is *Big Data*? Big Data is a set of high-volume, high-velocity, and high-variety information that demands cost-effective, innovative forms of information processing for enhanced insight and decision making.[1]

The end goal of Big Data should be to leverage the information resulting in increased value to the customer and an organization.

HOW BIG IS BIG? VOLUME LEVELS IN BIG DATA

In addition to transactional data and user-created data, the advent of the Internet opened the floodgates to new databases, new forms of data, and data that no longer needed to be created by human intervention.

DOMO.com created an analysis of the amount of data that is processed or created every minute over the Internet.[2] Consider the following by-the-minute volumes:

- YouTube users upload 400 hours of new video.
- Snapchat users watch 6,944,444 videos.
- Facebook messenger shares 216,302 photos.
- Amazon makes $222,283 in sales.
- Instagram users like 2,430,555 posts.
- Siri answers 99,206 requests.
- Dropbox users upload 833,333 new files.

From Internet Stats Live[3]

- Email users send 160,000,000 messages.[4]
- Twitter users tweet 450,793 times.
- Internet users in the world: 3,588,643,537
- Facebook active users: 1,867,648,665

---

[1] IT glossary, Gartner, www.gartner.com/ it-glossary/ big-data
[2] "Data Never Sleeps 4.0," https:// www.domo.com/ learn/ data-never-sleeps-4- 0 Accessed 3/ 28/ 17
[3] www.internetlivestats.com/ one-second/ # google-band, accessed 3/ 28/ 17
[4] Timed live at 7:35 p.m. on 3/ 15/ 2017, www.internetlivestats.com/ one-second/ # google-band

- Pinterest active users: 203,925,085
- Websites hacked: 63,345[5]

Just a couple of years ago, the number of global Internet users was estimated to be in excess of 2.4 billion people. Internet Stats Live estimates that there are now 3.6 billion global users.

The amount of data continues to grow exponentially. There's nothing on the horizon that suggests this increase of information will not continue. The challenge for the accountant is managing the expansion of information in terms of collecting, archiving, accessing, and interpreting. The growth in structured data, unstructured data, streaming data, and the like will only continue.

Why has everyone become so interested in the explosion of data that has become known as Big Data? The McKinsey Global Institute published research in 2011 in which it estimated that "retailers exploiting data analytics at scale across their organizations could increase their operating margins by more than 60 percent and that the U.S. healthcare sector could reduce costs by 8 percent through data-analytics efficiency and quality improvements."[6]

KNOWLEDGE CHECK

1. How can Big Data best be described?

    a. Large systems in multi-national companies.
    b. Structured data, unstructured data, and streaming data.
    c. Enterprise resource planning (ERP) systems with all software applications in the organization.
    d. Data processed with serial processing.

2. It is estimated that Snapchat users watch how many videos every minute of the day?

    a. Nearly 1 million.
    b. Nearly 4 million.
    c. Nearly 7 million
    d. Nearly 10 million.

---

[5] This figure is from 3/ 14/ 2017.
[6] David McCourt, "Getting Big Impact with Big Data," *McKinsey Quarterly*, January 2015, www.mckinsey.com/ insights/ business_technology/ getting_big_impact_from_big_data

EXAMPLES OF VOLUME

What type of data volumes does Big Data involve?

Table 1-1

Acronym	Description	Size
(B)	Byte	= 8 bits
(KB)	Kilobyte	= 1,000 bits
(MB)	Megabyte	= 1,000,000 bits
(GB)	Gigabyte	= 1,000,000,000 bits
(TB)	Terabyte	= 1,000,000,000,000 bits
(PB)	Petabyte	= 1,000,000,000,000,000 bits
(EB)	Exabyte	= 1,000,000,000,000,000,000 bits
(ZB)	Zettabyte	= 1,000,000,000,000,000,000,000 bits
(YB)	Yottabyte	= 1,000,000,000,000,000,000,000,000 bits

MEGABYTES, GIGABYTES, TERABYTES ... WHAT ARE THEY?

How much data could be contained in the preceding measurements? We turned to WhatsAByte.com to find out.[7]

Byte: 100 bytes equates to an average sentence like this one.

Kilobyte: 100 kilobytes equals a page of words like the one you're reading now.

Megabyte: 100 megabytes equals a couple volumes of encyclopedias. 600 megabytes is about the amount of data that will fit on a CD-ROM disk.

Gigabyte: 100 gigabytes could contain an entire library floor of academic journals.

Terabyte: A terabyte could hold 1,000 copies of the Encyclopedia Britannica. Ten terabytes could hold the printed collection of the Library of Congress.

---

[7] "Megabytes, Gigabytes, Terabytes...What Are They?" What's a Byte?, accessed 3/28/17, www.whatsabyte.com/

Petabyte: A petabyte could hold approximately 20 million four-door filing cabinets full of text. It could contain 500 billion pages of standard printed text.

Exabyte: It's estimated that five exabytes would be equal to all of the words ever spoken by mankind.

Zettabyte: 1 ZB is equivalent to approximately 152 million years of high-definition video.[8]

KNOWLEDGE CHECK

3. A petabyte could contain how many billion pages of standard text?

    a. 100.
    b. 500.
    c. 900.
    d. 750.

THE ACCOUNTANT AND BIG DATA

Although many organizations have sought to leverage Big Data applications and resources, they have not had the time or resources to pursue the dream fully. The American Productivity and Quality Center (APQC) conducted a study sponsored by Grant Thornton entitled "Financial Planning and Analysis: Influencing Corporate Performance with Stellar Processes, People, and Technology."[9] One of the study's conclusions was that the finance staff has not been at the forefront of the battle of Big Data. Two-thirds of survey respondents indicated that they spent too much time on basic financial management duties to improve financial planning and analysis. When asked what the most significant barriers to improving financial planning and analysis value to the business were, they responded as follows (see table 1-2):[10]

---

[8] www.economist.com/ news/ leaders/ 21707538-internet-not-american-whatever-ted-cruz-thinks-road-surfdom, accessed 3/ 28/ 17

[9] "Financial Planning and Analysis: Influencing Corporate Performance with Stellar Processes, People, and Technology," Grant Thornton website, March 23, 2015, www.grantthornton.com/ ~ / media/ content-page-files/ advisory/ pdfs/ 2015/ BAS-APQC-financial-planning-and-analysis-final.ashx, accessed 3/ 28/ 17

[10] Ibid. 11.

Table 1-2

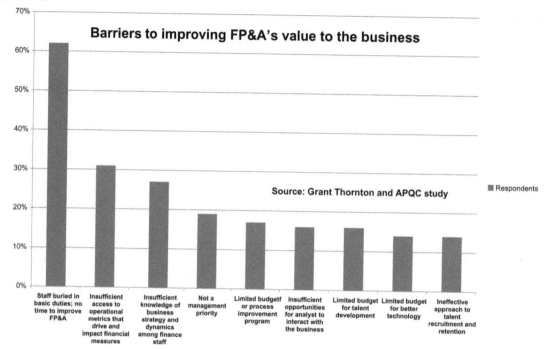

According to the study, "financial planning and analysis departments are consumed by the basics: data management, process administration, managing the machinery of periodic forecasting and variance analysis and working with the accounting staff to correct posting errors."

Having limited time to focus on data analysis, what were the major areas the financial planning and analysis group could focus on?

● Simple aggregation of exposures and losses	60 percent
● Basic cause-and-effect analysis	57 percent
● Scenarios and "what-if" analyses to identify possible outcomes	36 percent
● Predictive analysis techniques to project probable outcomes	24 percent

ACCOUNTING'S BIG DATA PROBLEM[11]

According to CFO.com, unless accountants and finance executives work for companies in businesses that provide or deliver data products and services, they may not be participants in the Big Data trend because most of them have been trained almost exclusively on structured data (data that fits into tables, Excel spreadsheets, databases, and the like) rather than unstructured data.

Keep in mind that unstructured data represents the most significant segment of existing data and will probably yield the largest benefit.

---

[11] Katz, David M., "Accounting's Big Data Problem," *CFO*, March 4, 2014, ww2.cfo.com/ management-accounting/ 2014/ 03/ accountings-big-data-problem/ , accessed 3/ 28/ 17

One such example of the unstructured data comes from Trax—a Singapore-based firm that provides an image-recognition app to gather data from photos taken of shelves at retail stores. The photos allow an organization to better manage inventories.

Another example of unstructured data can be found in corporations' published text in the following sources:

- 10-Ks and 10-Qs Management's Discussion and Analysis
- Press releases
- Interviews with corporate executives

BIG DATA TERMINOLOGY

As in any new field, Big Data has some terms that must be mastered. The following list is not meant to be all-inclusive, but it identifies many of the terms related to Big Data, analytics, and business intelligence.

Business intelligence (BI). The integration of data, technology, analytics, and human knowledge to optimize business decisions and ultimately drive an enterprise's success. BI programs usually combine an enterprise data warehouse and a BI platform or toolset to transform data into usable, actionable business information.[12]

Data analytics (DA). The science of examining raw data with the purpose of drawing conclusions from that information. Data analytics is used in many industries to allow companies and organizations to make better business decisions, and in the sciences to verify or disprove existing models or theories.[13]

Cloud computing. A model for delivering information technology services in which resources are retrieved from the Internet through web-based tools and applications rather than a direct connection to a server. Data and software packages are stored in servers. However, cloud computing allows access to information as long as an electronic device has access to the web. This type of system allows employees to work remotely.[14]

Dashboards. A business intelligence dashboard (BI dashboard) is a BI software interface that provides preconfigured or customer-defined metrics, statistics, insights, and visualization into current data. It allows the end and power users of BI software to view instant results into the live performance state of business or data analytics.[15]

Data mining. The practice of searching through large amounts of computerized data to find useful patterns or trends.[16]

---

[12] "Featured Education, Research and Resources," TDWI, https://tdwi.org Accessed 3/28/17
[13] "Data analytics," *TechTarget*, Accessed 3/28/17, searchdatamanagement.techtarget.com/definition/data-analytics
[14] "Cloud computing," *Investopedia*, Accessed 3/28/17, www.investopedia.com/terms/c/cloud-computing.asp
[15] "Dashboards," *Techopedia*, Accessed 3/28/17, www.techopedia.com/definition/13773/business-intelligence-dashboard-bi-dashboard
[16] "Data mining," *Merriam-Webster's Collegiate Dictionary*, 11th edition, Springfield, MA, Merriam Webster, 2003. Also available at www.merriamwebster.com.

Data scientist. An employee or BI consultant who excels at analyzing data, particularly large amounts of data, to help a business gain a competitive edge.[17]

Data visualization. The presentation of data in a pictorial or graphic format.

Hadoop. A free, java-based programming framework that supports the processing of large data sets in a distributed computing environment. It is part of the Apache project, sponsored by the Apache Software Foundation.[18]

OLAP. (OnLine Analytical Processing). OLAP is a powerful technology for data discovery, including capabilities for limitless report viewing, complex analytical calculations, and predictive "what-if" scenario (budget, forecast) planning.[19]

Predictive analytics. The practice of extracting information from existing data sets to determine patterns and predict future outcomes and trends. Predictive analytics does not tell you what will happen in the future. It forecasts what might happen in the future with an acceptable level of reliability, and includes what-if scenarios and risk assessment.[20]

Prescriptive analytics. A type of business analytics that focuses on finding the best course of action for a given situation and belongs to a portfolio of analytic capabilities that include descriptive and predictive analytics.[21]

Semi-structured data. Data that has not been organized into a specialized repository, such as a database, but that nevertheless has associated information, such as metadata, that makes it more amenable to processing than raw or unstructured data. For example, a Word document contains metadata or tagging that allows for keyword searches, but it does not have as much relational structure or utility as the information in a database.[22]

Structured data. Data that resides in a fixed field within a record or file. This includes data contained in relational databases and spreadsheets.[23]

Unstructured data. Information that doesn't reside in a traditional row-column database. It often includes text and multimedia. Examples include email messages, word processing documents, videos, photos, audio files, presentations, web pages, and many other kinds of business documents. Although these files may have an internal structure, they are considered "unstructured" because the data is not contained in a database. Experts estimate that 80 percent to 90 percent of the data in any organization is unstructured.[24]

---

[17] "Data scientist," *TechTarget*, Accessed 3/ 28/ 17, searchbusinessanalytics.techtarget.com/ definition/ Data-scientist
[18] Ibid., "Hadoop," *TechTarget*, searchcloudcomputing.techtarget.com/ definition/ Hadoop
[19] "OLAP," *OLAP.com*, Accessed 3/ 28/ 17, olap.com/ olap-definition/
[20] "Predictive analytics," *Webopedia*, Accessed 3/ 28/ 17, www.webopedia.com/ TERM/ P/ predictive_analytics.html
[21] "Prescriptive analytics," *TechTarget*, Accessed 3/ 28/ 17, searchcio.techtarget.com/ definition/ Prescriptive-analytics
[22] Ibid., "Semi-structured data," whatis.techtarget.com/ definition/ semi-structured-data, whatis.techtarget.com/ definition/ semi-structured-data
[23] "Structured data," *Webopedia*, whatis.techtarget.com/ definition/ semi-structured-data, www.webopedia.com/ TERM/ S/ structured_data.html
[24] Ibid., "Unstructured data," whatis.techtarget.com/ definition/ semi-structured-data, www.webopedia.com/ TERM/ U/ unstructured_data.html

FOUR TYPES OF DATA ANALYTICS

Adding to the examples and sources of Big Data, let's examine how some of the definitions and related terminology we've just learned fit into processes used to examine data. Different types of analytics can be used to analyze Big Data for different purposes.

Descriptive Analytics

Descriptive analytics is information that has happened in the past. From an accounting perspective, this would represent traditional historical financial information. Consider the following examples:

- An assessment of customer credit risk can be predicted based on that company's past financial performance.
- A prediction of sales results can be created from customers' product preferences and sales cycle.
- Current product reviews can be used to predict future sales.
- Employee evaluation can be used to predict turnover.

Diagnostic Analytics

Diagnostic analysis describes the reason for the historical results. It attempts to answer the question "Why did this happen?" as in the following examples:

- In traditional finance, variance analysis uncovers the underlying reasons for differences in budgeted and actual results.
- Causal analysis can be used to describe why certain results occurred.
- Analytic dashboards can be used to describe why something happened. For example, during the Ebola outbreak in Africa, it was possible to view the daily spread of the virus as it occurred in different geographic regions.
- Tracking the increase in views, posts, fans, followers, and so forth, as a result of purchasing additional views on Facebook to increase the exposure of a particular post, video, or picture.

Discovery Analysis (Insight)

Although not technically one of the four types of data analytics, the step of discovery analysis could be inserted between diagnostic and predictive analytics. During discovery analysis or insight, research and analysis can be undertaken to identify whether there is a relationship between the historical information and another database.

Predictive Analytics

Predictive analytics attempts to determine what will happen by analyzing historical data and trends. Consider the following examples of predictive analytics:

- An accounting department prepares a cash flow projection report.
- Preparing an estimate of inventory levels
- Predicting an outcome based on changed assumptions. The revenue will increase by a specific percentage if an additional 5 percent is spent on the marketing budget.
- The issuance of additional coupons or promotions for a retail organization is projected to result in a 10 percent increase in revenue.
- Based on historical results, ads released the week of Black Friday are predicted to generate greater than normal sales for the Black Friday holiday shopping season.

Here is another well-known example of predictive analytics from the sports world:

> During the early 2000s, the New York Yankees were the most acclaimed team in Major League Baseball. But on the other side of the continent, the Oakland A's were racking up success after success, with much less fanfare—and much less money.
>
> While the Yankees paid its star players tens of millions, the A's managed to be successful with a low payroll. How did they do it? When signing players, they didn't just look at basic productivity values such as RBIs, home runs, and earned-run averages. Instead, they analyzed hundreds of detailed statistics from every player and every game, attempting to predict future performance and production. Some statistics were even obtained from videos of games using video recognition techniques. This allowed the team to sign great players who may have been lesser-known, but who were equally productive on the field. The A's started a trend, and predictive analytics began to penetrate the world of sports with a splash, with copycats using similar techniques.[25]

Perhaps predictive analytics will someday help bring Major League salaries into line.

There are tools that can also be used as part of the predictive analysis. One such example that will be addressed in a later chapter is the Net Promoter Score. The Net Promoter Score provides an indication of how willing a customer is to promote or recommend your products, on a scale of 1–10. Companies want to achieve a 9 or 10 with each customer. At this level, the customer will be "promoting" your product to other potential customers.

Prescriptive Analytics

Prescriptive analytics uses the information from descriptive, diagnostic, and predictive analytics to suggest specific decisions or changes in approach to a business strategy. It could also be described as the best scenario to take to achieve the desired outcome. The following are examples of prescriptive data analytics:

- Airline seat prices and the manner in which the cost per seat regularly increases as the departure date draws near. A related component of this decision is the airlines' decision to overbook flights and offer incentives to placate passengers who are inconvenienced.
- Applications such as Facebook suggest to the user that there are additional friends they may wish to connect with. This "prescription for connecting" is based on the analysis of common friends in both of the individuals' profiles. Hence, the new friends and our potential friends are suggested as contacts.
- The most common prescriptive analytics would be medical drugs that have been known to alleviate certain medical issues (statin drugs, diabetic drugs, blood pressure drugs, and the like). The medications can also have negative predictions due to potential problem interactions.

---

[25] "Predictive Analytics: A Primer," *Amberoon*, accessed 3/ 28/ 17, www.amberoon.com/ CarpeDatumRx/ bid/ 236799/ Predictive-Analytics-A-Primer

BENEFITS OF BIG DATA

Now that you know what Big Data is, you may be wondering how it will help you in your practice. What are the benefits an organization can derive from Big Data? A study from IBM[26] showed that organizations competing on analytics outperform competitors by:

- 1.6 x revenue growth
- 2.5 x stock price appreciation
- 2.0 x EBITDA (earnings before interest, taxes, depreciation and amortization) growth.

Also, the World Economic Forum in 2012 stated that data gathering is a new class of economic asset, like currency and gold.

What are the benefits of Big Data?

Big Data offers strategic benefits for businesses, including the following:

- Better strategic decisions
- Quicker arrival of new products and services to market
- Increased innovation
- Better insight into the business
- Better insight into the competition
- Real-time change for existing products, services, or offers
- Environmental scans for threats or opportunities

Big Data also aids in decision capability enhancement such as the following:

- Increase retained and analyzed amount of data
- Increase the speed of data analysis
- Produce more accurate results
- Better decision-making processes
- Improved forecasting
- More accurate identification of root cause analysis
- Smarter decisions—leverage new sources of data to improve the quality of decision-making
- Faster decisions—enabled more real-time data capture and analysis to support decision-making at the point of impact, such as when a customer is navigating our website or on the telephone with a customer service representative
- Decisions that make a difference—focus Big Data efforts toward areas that provide true differentiation
- Analysis based on entire data sets as opposed to sample sets
- Enhanced transparency of data

Businesses will also experience efficiency improvements, including the following:

- Reduce or eliminate manual processes
- Cost savings
- Increased productivity
- Automated routine decisions

---

[26] "Analytics: The Real-World Use of Big Data," IBM, Accessed 3/28/17, www.ibm.com/ services/ us/ gbs/ thoughtleadership/ ibv-big-data-at-work.html

- Improved manufacturing productivity and maintenance
- Integration of previously related databases
- Improved scalability

Customer relationships and sales can also benefit from utilizing Big Data. Some of the benefits in these areas include the following:

- Improved customer satisfaction
- Better customer service
- Increased input from customers
- Improved sales results via cross-selling and upselling
- Increased attraction and retention of customers
- Increased targeted marketing via social media

Finally, Big Data can enhance a business's governance and compliance efforts through the following:

- Improved fraud detection
- Improved risk assessment and management
- Tools that can scan and access corporate data to prevent unauthorized release of data

KNOWLEDGE CHECK

4. Describe decision making within a Big Data framework.

    a. Smarter, faster, more accurate.
    b. Slower, more detailed, more structured.
    c. Slower, more accurate, more transparent.
    d. Same speed, more accurate, more structured.

Practice Questions

1. What are the components of Big Data?

2. What are the four stages of analytics?

3. What is Hadoop?

4. Describe what a data scientist does.

Chapter 2

BIG DATA HISTORY—BIG DATA SOURCES AND CHARACTERISTICS

LEARNING OBJECTIVES

After completing this chapter, you should be able to do the following:

- Identify distinctive points of computing history and their impact on the evolution of Big Data today.
- Identify Big Data sources.
- Recall Big Data from the perspectives of a small business and the accountant.

INTRODUCTION

This chapter examines the history as well as the sources and characteristics of Big Data. To accountants, the concept of Big Data relates to the ability to access, manipulate, analyze, and report on data using tools such as electronic spreadsheets. Understanding the history of computing and the evolution from clay tablets to modern day computer systems is essential. To best employ Big Data, we must recognize the past, present, and future implications of Big Data for our organizations as well as our profession.

Big Data can be created in a multitude of ways and transformed into knowledge by many avenues, providing that the organization has the skills and resources to do so. It is also important to recognize that data can be identified by a variety of characteristics.

THE ACCOUNTANT'S PERSPECTIVE—BIG DATA = SPREADSHEETS

Prior to 1978, the accountant's job was a factor of the underlying accounting systems. The accountant recorded, processed, and analyzed transactions and reported on the financial results. Also, the accountant created additional value by evaluating results based on ratio and variance analysis and industry comparisons. In 1978, the world's first spreadsheet, VisiCalc, was created. As a result, accountants began to input transactional data into spreadsheets and create new analyses. Spreadsheets resulted in customized reports and an increase in the overall volume of data. Over the last three decades, spreadsheet usage has increased. Database applications and large enterprise systems have become more available, user-friendly, accessible, and powerful. The accountant who was data-challenged prior to 1978 is today awash with so much data that it has become overwhelming. Accountants drown in data, but they lack the knowledge that is hidden in the data stream.

BIG DATA FROM THE ACCOUNTANT'S PERSPECTIVE

Accountants tend to look at data from their traditional data perspectives of acquiring, gathering, categorizing, aggregating, analyzing, and reporting information. Larger systems facilitated integrated and more complex analysis. The availability of Big Data allows for increased complexity and an increased ability to perform deep data analysis which was not possible previously.

Figure 2-1

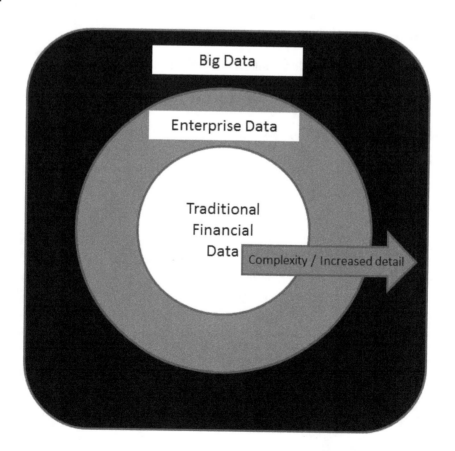

KNOWLEDGE CHECK

1. What was the first spreadsheet developed in 1978?

    a. Lotus.
    b. Excel.
    c. VisiCalc.
    d. Multi-mate.

HISTORY

When the history of Big Data is viewed through the lens of accounting, it can be categorized by the interaction of seven different areas:

- Bookkeeping
- Accounting
- Calculating machines
- Computers
- Internet
- Cloud computing
- Internet of things

Each of these seven areas has been built upon or interacted with the other categories to result in the current access and application of Big Data. Consider some of the significant occurrences within each of the categories as they paved the way for Big Data. The first three categories remind us from where we came. As you consider the fourth through fifth categories, jot down the impact that any of the items has made for you or your company.

Bookkeeping

Bookkeeping has been a part of human civilization from the very beginnings of recorded history. Chaldean-Babylonian civilization is attributed with having the first formal bookkeeping or recordkeeping activities. Archaeological evidence of the code of Hammurabi (leader of Babylonia from 2285–2242 B.C.) includes the following:

> 104. If a merchant gives an agent corn, wool, oil, or any other goods to transport, the agent shall give a receipt for the amount, and compensate the merchant therefor. Then he shall obtain a receipt [from] the merchant for the money that he gives the merchant.

> 105. If the agent is careless and does not take a receipt for the money which he gave the merchant, he cannot consider the unreceipted money as his own.

106. If the agent accepts money from the merchant but has a quarrel with the merchant (denying the receipt), then shall the merchant swear before God and witnesses that he has given this money to the agent, and the agent shall pay him three times the sum.[1]

In the earliest civilizations, transactions were recorded on clay tablets. During Egyptian times, transactions were recorded on papyrus. Systems continued evolving through Greek, Roman, and Israeli civilizations. Eventually, to promote accountability of officials, public accounts were chiseled into stone. Records were used to facilitate transactions, tax assessment, and payment.

KNOWLEDGE CHECK

2. Among the earliest historical evidence of the need for transaction recording was

    a. The Roman tax code.
    b. Code of Hammurabi.
    c. Greek merchant records.
    d. Chinese trade records.

Accounting

In 1494, Fra Luca Pacioli (who wrote and taught in the fields of mathematics, theology, architecture, games, military strategy, and commerce) published *Summa de Arithmetica, Geometria, Proportioni et Proportionalita* (*The Collected Knowledge of Arithmetic, Geometry, Proportion and Proportionality*). A section of the book contained a treatise on bookkeeping, a section that ensured Pacioli a place in history as "The Father of Accounting," although he did not invent the practice of accounting—but rather described the process of double-entry accounting, known as the method of Venice.[2]

His system included most of the accounting cycle as we know it today. He published information on the use of journals and ledgers and described the process of debits and credits, including the fact that debits should equal credits. "As Pacioli says, this is the most important thing to note in Venetian bookkeeping: 'All creditors must appear in the ledger at the right-hand side and all the debtors on the left. All entries made in the ledger have to be double entries—that is, if you make one creditor, you must make someone debtor."[3]

His ledger included assets, which included receivables, and inventories, liabilities, capital, income, and expense accounts. The *Summa* was eventually translated into German, Russian, Dutch, and English.

Pacioli's system is the basis for the accounting systems still in use today. Fundamentally, not much has changed, even through the Industrial Revolution and the rise of corporations. However, a pivotal event in the American history of accounting came in 1913 when the Sixteenth Amendment was ratified. The amendment required a federal income tax to be paid by all individuals working in the United States.

---

[1] "The Code of Hammurabi," translation by L.W. King, Yale Law School website, http://avalon.law.yale.edu/ancient/hamframe.asp, accessed 3/29/17
[2] Jane Gleeson-White, "Luca Pacioli's double entry and the birth of financial management," November 11, 2012, *Financial Management*, www.fm-magazine.com/feature/depth/luca-pacioli%E2%80%99s-double-entry-and-birth-financial-management#, accessed 3/29/17
[3] Ibid.

Income tax and corporate tax were little understood and heavily resisted in their formative years. As a result, most corporations and individuals were simply not filing or were filing incorrectly.

A few years later in 1917, the Federal Reserve published *Uniform Accounting*, a document that attempted to set industry standards for how financials should be organized both for reporting tax and for financial statements.

Calculating Machines

The history of calculating machines is nearly as old as the history of bookkeeping. The first calculating machine, the abacus, was in use as early as 2400 B.C.

The early calculators of the 17ᵗʰ century laid the foundation for the computing revolution that would take place centuries later. Tabulating machines have been used by the accounting profession since the 1800s. A few key dates from a photographic timeline on Gizmodo are outlined as follows:[4]

- 1642: The Pascaline or Pascal's Calculator, by Blaise Pascal. It could add, subtract, multiply and divide two numbers.
- 1820: The Arithmométre, the first mass-produced mechanical calculator, by Charles Xavier Thomas de Colmar.
- 1800s: The difference engines, the first mechanical computers, by Charles Babbage in the early 1800s
- 1948: The hand-cranked calculator Curta, invented by Curt Herzstark. Type II was introduced in 1954 and produced until 1972.
- 1971: Sharp Corporation invents the pocket calculator.

Computers

The advent of modern computers took place in the 20th century. It revolutionized the accounting profession through increased speed, automation, and the introduction of spreadsheets. Although most of us witnessed much of the evolution first-hand, a timeline of key dates is outlined as follows:

- 1911: IBM is created.
- 1938: The Z1 computer was created, Konrad Zuse. It was a binary digital computer that used punch tape.
- 1947: William Shockley invents the transistor at Bell Labs.
- 1958: Advanced Research Projects Agency (ARPA) and NASA are formed.
  The first integrated circuit, or silicon chip, is produced by Jack Kilby and Robert Noyce.
- 1971: Ray Tomlinson invents email.
  Liquid crystal display (LCD) is developed by James Fergason.
  The floppy disk is created by David Noble with IBM. It is nicknamed the "floppy" for its flexibility.
- 1973: The Ethernet, a local-area network (LAN) protocol, is developed by Robert Metcalfe and David Boggs.

  The minicomputer Xerox Alto was a landmark step in the development of personal computers.

- 1977: Apple Computer's Apple II, the first personal computer with color graphics, is demonstrated.

  Ward Christensen writes the "MODEM" program, allowing two microcomputers to exchange files over a phone line.

---

[4] Vincze Miklós, "The History of Early Computing Machines, from Ancient Times to 1981," *iO9/ Gizmodo*, accessed 3/ 29/ 17, io9.gizmodo.com/ the-history-of-early-computing-machines-from-ancient-t-549202742

- 1980: IBM hires Paul Allen and Bill Gates to create an operating system for a new PC. They buy the rights to a simple operating system manufactured by Seattle Computer Products and use it as a template to develop DOS.

Internet

Considering how integral the Internet is to everyday life, it's hard to believe it's less than 50 years old. In 1969, the U.S. Department of Defense set up the Advanced Research Projects Agency Network (ARPANET) with the intention of creating a computer network that could withstand any disaster. It became the first building block for what the Internet has become today.

In 1990, Tim Berners-Lee and Robert Cailliau proposed HTML hypertext protocol for the Internet and World Wide Web. That same year, the first commercial Internet dial-up access provider came online. The next year, the World Wide Web was launched to the public.

A few more key dates in the development of the Internet:

- 1994: The World Wide Web Consortium is founded by Tim Berners-Lee to help with the development of common protocols for the evolution of the World Wide Web.

  Yahoo! is created.

- 1995: Java is introduced.

  Jeff Bezos launches Amazon.com.

  Pierre Omidyar begins eBay.

  Jack Smith and Sabeer Bhatia create Hotmail.

- 1998: Sergey Brin and Larry Page begin Google.

  Peter Thiel and Max Levchin start PayPal.

- Apple PowerBook G3 released.
- 2001: Bill Gates introduces the Xbox.

  Windows XP is launched.

- 2005: Blu-ray Discs are introduced.

  YouTube gets its start.

- 2009: Windows 7 released.
- 2012: Microsoft Windows 8 and Microsoft Surface are released.

Cloud Computing

Cloud computing is one of the newest developments in the use of the Internet. Instead of maintaining data and software on individual computers or local servers, data and programs can now be accessed in the "cloud." The term "cloud" was coined in 1997 to refer to the concept of shared data services and third-party access. Other recent developments in cloud computing are the formation of Amazon web services in 2002, Application Service Providers (ASPs) in 2005, and Hadoop in 2006.

The "Internet of Things" refers to the "network of Internet-connected objects able to collect and exchange data."[5] Each object has a unique identifier and the ability to communicate machine-to-machine, without any human interaction. For instance, your home's intruder alert system automatically sends a signal when a lock is broken. The following is a brief timeline of the "Internet of Things":[6, 7, 8]

- 1832: Baron Schilling of Russia invents the electromagnetic telegraph. A year later, Germans Carl Friedrich Gauss and Wilhelm Weber invent a code to communicate over a distance of 1,200 meters.
- 1961: GM introduces first industrial robot—Unimate—in New Jersey factory.
- 1969: ARPANET connects UCLA and Stanford universities.
- 1970: The Stanford Cart is unveiled, becoming the first "smart car." Built for lunar exploration, it is controlled remotely and features a wireless video camera.
- The first hand-held mobile cellphone goes on the market. It weighs 4.4. pounds.
- 1973: The first read-write radio frequency identification (RFID) tag is patented by Mario Cardullo. RFID tags will eventually lead to the wireless sensors so critical for enterprise, industrial and manufacturing IoT technologies.
- 1993: The first webcam is created to monitor a coffee pot.
- 1994: Bluetooth is invented as an alternative to data cables to connect keyboards and phones to computers.
- 1999: Kevin Ashton, executive director of MIT's Auto-ID Center, coins the term "Internet of Things."
- 2000: Global Positioning System (GPS) becomes widely used by the public.
- 2001: Auto-ID Center proposes electronic product code to identify every object in the world uniquely.
- 2005: Arduino simplifies interconnecting devices.
- 2006: Hadoop developed.
- 2010: Bluetooth low energy (BLE) is introduced, enabling applications in the fitness, health care, security, and home entertainment industries.
- 2011: Nest Labs introduces sensor-driven, Wi-Fi-enabled, self-learning, programmable thermostats and smoke detectors.
- 2011: Internet Protocol version 6 (IPv6) expands the number of objects that can connect to the Internet by introducing 340 undecillion IP addresses.[9]
- 2014: Apple announces HealthKit and HomeKit, two health and home automation developments. The company's iBeacon advances context and geolocation services. [10]

---

[5] "The Internet of Things" infographic, *Business Insider,* April 13, 2016, www.businessinsider.com/ iot-ecosystem-internet-of-things-forecasts-and-business-opportunities-2016-2?utm_source= feedly&utm_medium= webfeeds

[6] Jennifer Duval, "Timeline of The Internet of Things," *HSTRY,* accessed 3/ 29/ 17, edu.hstry.co/ timeline/ timeline-of-the-internet-of-things

[7] Gil Press, "A Very Short History of the Internet of Things." *Forbes,* June 18, 2014, www.forbes.com/ sites/ gilpress/ 2014/ 06/ 18/ a-very-short-history-of-the-internet-of-things/ 2/ #704ac6176343, accessed 3/ 29/ 17

[8] Michael Kanellos, "Can Apple Alums Make a Thermostat Hip?" *Forbes,* October 25, 2011, www.forbes.com/ sites/ michaelkanellos/ 2011/ 10/ 25/ nest-labs-can-apple-alums-make-a-thermostat-hip/ # 1e52e94271e2, accessed 3/ 29/ 17

[9] Hansi Lo Wang, "IPv6: A New Internet Expands the Web by Trillions of Addresses," June 6, 2012, *NPR,* www.npr.org/ sections/ alltechconsidered/ 2012/ 06/ 06/ 154430791/ ipv6-a-new-internet-expands-the-web-by-trillions-of-addresses, accessed 3/ 29/ 17

[10] "Internet of Things: Patent Landscape Analysis," LexInnova report, 2015, WIPO, www.wipo.int/ edocs/ plrdocs/ en/ internet_of_things.pdf, accessed 3/ 29/ 17

Now that you're familiar with the history and rapid development of certain areas of technology, let's take a look at the seven categories we just learned about and the key characteristics of their data volume, information preparation, and the type of data analysis conducted. These categories and characteristics are especially interesting when accountants consider the implications for future accounting careers. A large component of the accounting position was preparation and massaging numbers for decision-making purposes. Big Data may eliminate many of the lower level accounting positions due to making the preparation and massaging of numbers unnecessary.

Table 2-1: Evolution of Recordkeeping to Computing to Today's Big Data

Description	Volume of data	How information is (was) created	What type of data analysis?
Bookkeeping	Low/transaction	Manual	No time
Accounting	Low/transaction	Manual	Minimal time/manual reports
Calculating Machines	Medium/transaction	Manual/small automation	Minimal time/manual reports
Computers	High/transaction/reporting	Manual/high automation	Volumes of automated structured analysis
Internet	High/transaction/reporting	Manual/high automation	Volumes of automated structured analysis + data detectives to find corroborating or competitive data
Cloud	High/transaction/reporting	Manual/high automation	Volumes of automated structured analysis + volumes of unstructured data + data detectives to find corroborating or competitive data + predictive tools to analyze volumes of data
Internet of Things	Unlimited/unstructured	Automatically generated sensors, and the like	Volumes of automated structured analysis + volumes of unstructured data + data detectives to find corroborating or competitive data + predictive tools to analyze volumes of data + automated applications to gather, archive, evaluate and predict data patterns, trends and strategic actions

KNOWLEDGE CHECK

3. Who is credited with creating the first building block of what the Internet is today?

    a. UCLA.
    b. The U.S. Department of Defense.
    c. Stanford.
    d. Harvard.

EXAMINE BIG DATA THROUGH THE EYES OF A SMALL BUSINESS

Next, we will consider an example of a landscaping business. What are the ways that it could leverage sources of Big Data to produce additional insights into the operations, the financial operations, and the customer?

Let us imagine that you are the owner of a landscaping business with fewer than 50 employees. Without any great insight into accounting or management theories, you began the business with just some equipment and a truck. The sum total of your equipment was limited to the truck, trailer, and commercial lawn mower. You went out and obtained customers using a fixed fee approach based on your best guess of what the customer was willing to pay. You worked from sunup to sundown loading your lawn mower on your trailer, driving to your customers, unloading the lawn mower, performing the mowing services and then started again the next day. At the end of any given week, month, or landscaping season, you judged the success of your business based on the remaining cash in your account. The business was simple. You were the only employee. Your expenses were for gasoline, repairs and maintenance, minimal advertising, and minimal professional help. As your landscaping business grew, you hired employees, purchased more equipment and hoped that the additional investment in employees and equipment would result in a larger increase in cash profits.

As an owner, you eventually implemented financial and operational systems to make the business a little more sophisticated. Although still concerned with cash, you are now receiving regular financial statements from an accounting firm. You are operating as the typical small business with employees—struggling to find customers, operate the business, meet financial obligations, and pay yourself.

The following chart describes operating the small business in the normal course of events. How could the lawn maintenance business have capitalized on Big Data concepts to improve the business?

Table 2-2: Lawn Mowing—Landscape Business Example

Current Business	With Big Data
Worker picks up truck, trailer, and mower at business location	Have the employee text his starting time (which could be verified)
Fills truck and mower with gas	
Drives to customer	Could optimize the traffic pattern, track the actual route (deviations), monitor vital truck signs
Unloads equipment	Could track time to unload mower
Cuts lawn	Could track cutting pattern with gaps, hours driven, miles traveled, the speed of the machine; could track music being played, could track downtime of the engine. Could take a photo of completed work—four standard pictures.
Reloads mower	Could track time to load mower
Drives to next customer (repeat process)	Could optimize the traffic pattern, track the actual route (deviations), monitor vital truck signs
Returns truck, trailer, and mower to business location	Could record time in and take photo of condition of equipment
What do we normally get as data?	**What could we get as data?**
Starting time (time card) at work	Detailed time analysis of all steps
Arrival time at customer	Mechanical evaluations of all equipment
Departure time from customer	Mechanical evaluation from mower can be evaluated and used as predictive measure of quality
Arrival time back at work	Music can be compared to timeliness, quality of job
Ending time (time card) leaving work	Photos can document the condition of equipment at the start and end of the day. Can also document the quality of lawn care.
	Photos can also be used as customer survey, proof of service, or testimonial
Customers are billed for a fixed fee for mowing the lawn	

Table 2-2: Lawn Mowing—Landscape Business Example (continued)

The owner knows profitability based on the following:	With multiple jobs, we can now better assess time and cost for each job.
Cost of gas for tractor	We can assess the quality of jobs and quality of employees.
Cost of gas for truck	We can establish improved metrics for current customers.
Hourly costs for worker	If multiple mowing assignments with multiple employees, better benchmarks can be established.
Depreciation of equipment	Warning signs of any mechanical failures can be addressed prior to their occurrence.
Maintenance of equipment	Photos can also be used to monitor the actual time worked.
The owner determines his quotes based on 20 years of experience and competitor pricing	The owner assessed quotes based on his experience and increased access to Big Data

Small businesses may be limited in their ability to pursue Big Data opportunities. However, the expense is usually not prohibitive, and the information (when used appropriately) can make the company more efficient, productive and profitable.

Also, based on the preceding example, the owner of the landscape business could analyze many Big Data opportunities as well as customer behavior including payments, timeliness of payments, renewal dates, social media comments, and net promoter scores.

BIG DATA SOURCES

There are a variety of Big Data information sources that an organization can access. Consider table 2-3, which breaks down the sources of data among five different categories:

Table 2-3: Sources of Data

Customer data Vendor data Product data Shipping data Accounting data Marketing data Employee data	Traffic count Attendees Number of calls RFID	Emails Surveys PDFs PowerPoints Documents Pictures Video Audio Consultant Info	Industry data Government data Almanac Benchmarking	Twitter LinkedIn Facebook Google search info Web RFID GPS Internet of Things Pictures Video Audio Edgar Industry data Government data Consultant info

Table 2-4: Reporting and Processing of Data

Known structured data	Known, unused structured data	Known unstructured data	Unknown structured data	Unknown unstructured data
Traditional IT systems	Identification	Analytics	Acquisition	Acquisition
Excel Database Reporting Forecasting	Catalog Curate Relate Predict	Identification Catalog Curate Relate Predict	Catalog Curate Relate Predict	Analytics Identification Catalog Curate Relate Predict

Note in the preceding tables that the sources of data are broken down into five major categories:

1. Structured data that the company has
2. Structured data that the company has but has not developed
3. Unstructured data that the organization has
4. Structured data that the organization does not have
5. Unstructured data that the organization does not have

Accountants are very familiar with the first and fourth categories mentioned. These categories are typically represented by traditional accounting and financial applications. Also, these categories are used to perform ratio and interpretive analysis to provide insight or understanding to structured data within these systems. Some companies may have explored the use of category two items (unused structured data that they have) especially if they have developed areas of emphasis such as key performance indicators. The real challenge is for the organization to leverage categories three and five (unstructured data.)

In table 2-4, the tools required to access each of the categories are outlined as follows:

- In category one, reporting and processing involve traditional accounting accumulation, reporting, forecasting, and analysis.
- Category two requires the organization to identify what information is necessary to provide insight into the organization. Once identified, the company must catalog the information to allow access to it. The curator process prunes the necessary information and discards that which is not desired. Lastly, the information is related to other financial information to determine if it can be used to infer some impact on the financial performance of the organization.
- Tools that can be used in the third category assess unstructured data that the organization has not considered before but currently has access to. Typically, the organization will run analysis to determine if the data are valuable for further analysis. If so, the organization follows the same pattern as category two.
- In the fourth category, tools must identify structured data that is available outside of the organization but not collected. Once identified, it must be collected, transformed, or related to other existing data and analyzed for insights. An example of this would be obtaining industrial production statistics on a monthly basis and comparing that information with the monthly sales to determine if there is any correlation. The monthly industrial production statistics would also be made available for regular analysis of the organization activities (for example, sales).
- The fifth category represents unstructured data that the organization does not have and that the organization does not know the value of. In this category, the organization must first acquire the unstructured data and, once acquired, evaluate with analytics to determine if there is any value in the data to predict the financial impact on the organization.

SOURCES OF BIG DATA

Sources of Big Data are everywhere. You are probably aware of a few of these sources, such as Facebook, LinkedIn, and other large social media sites that many people use daily. However, you might not realize that sites like Facebook and LinkedIn use every feature of the site, including your posts, messages, photos, and searches, to collect data. Other sources of Big Data include the following:

- Google searches
- Email databases

- Retail customer relationship management (CRM)
- Health records, including insurance, hospital, mental health, prisons
- Forums
- Social media
- Twitter
- RFID tags
- GPS-enabled devices
- Smart meters
- YouTube
- Government databases
- Amazon.com
- Cross-selling

Do you know what the largest source of Big Data is? According to an IBM survey, the major source of Big Data that is currently being tracked is transactions. The rest of the survey results are depicted in table 2-5.[11]

Table 2-5

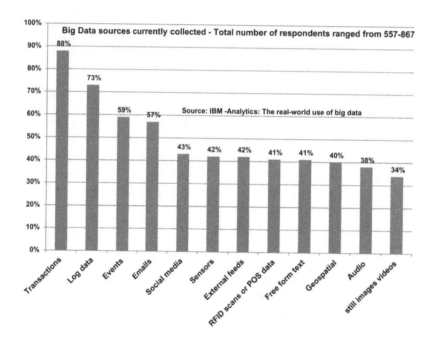

Another major source of Big Data comes from the Information of Things that is collected from objects, animals, and people. The activities or tools that generate Big Data are depicted in table 2-6 using information gathered from a Vitria survey.[12]

---

[11] "Analytics: The Real-World Use of Big Data," IBM, 11, accessed 3/29/17, www.ibm.com/ smarterplanet/ global/ files/ se__sv_se__intelligence__Analytics_-_The_real-world_use_of_big_data.pdf

[12] "Real-Time Big Data Analytics + Internet of Things = Value Creation," Vitria,January 2015, www.vitria.com/ infographics/ 2015-real-time-big-data-analytics-and-iot-infographic, accessed 3/ 29/ 17

Table 2-6

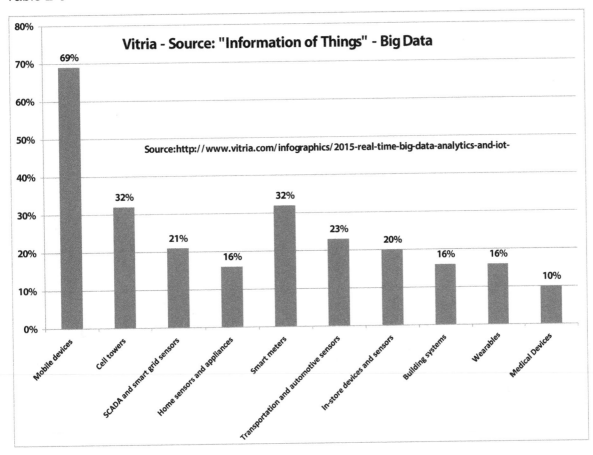

CHARACTERISTICS OF BIG DATA

The Four Dimensions of Big Data

Analysts have broken down Big Data into four dimensions to help organizations understand that challenges in big data management come from the expansion of all four properties, not just volume alone. These dimensions are what distinguished Big Data from traditional sources of information contained in a historical or enterprise-wide system.

1. Volume: The quantity of data which is generated every second, minute, hour, and day. The size of data created per day is increasing from gigabytes to terabytes and then petabytes. By 2020, IBM estimates that 40 zettabytes of information will be created by the year 2020.[13]
2. Velocity: Speed at which data is generated and processed. The ability to tap into streaming data to make predictions within seconds. IBM estimates that by 2016, 18.9 billion network connections that represent almost 2. 5 connections for each person on the globe.[14]
3. Variety: The different types of data that are widely available. The data can be structured, unstructured, text, and multimedia. There were estimated to be 420 million wearable, wireless health

---

[13] "The Four V's of Big Data" infographic, IBM, accessed 3/ 39/ 17, bigdatahub.com/ infographic/ four-vs-big-data
[14] Ibid.

monitors and that more than 4 billion hours of video will be watched on YouTube each month by 2014.[15]

4. Veracity: How reliable or accurate the data are. Currently, there exist levels of uncertainty and reliability. Managing the reliability and uncertainty of imprecise data will be essential.

KNOWLEDGE CHECK

4. What was the estimated number of wearable, wireless health monitors projected to be in 2014?

    a. 240 million.
    b. 360 million.
    c. 420 million.
    d. 500 million.

More Characteristics of Big Data

The scope of Big Data is large, and the goal is to capture as much of the population as possible, as opposed to small data sets. Ideally, the data have these characteristics: detailed, relational, and flexible. The data should be in great detail with the ability to index significant sub-parts of the data which can be used for discovery and predictive purposes. The data should be relational, allowing the ability to connect fields from different data sets. The data should be flexible so that it is not difficult to add additional fields or additional data (increased volume.)

Table 2-7

Characteristic	Small data	Big Data
Volume	Limited to large	Very large, entire populations
Exhaustivity	Samples	Entire populations
Resolution and Identification	Course and weak to tight and strong	Tight and strong
Relationality	Weak to strong	Strong
Velocity	Slow, freeze-framed or bundled	Fast, continuous
Variety	Limited to wide	Wide
Flexible and scalable	Low to middling	High

---

[15] Ibid.

EXAMPLE: RETAIL SURVEY

Let's assume that we run a retail store with multiple locations. The store sells a variety of pet products including supplies, food, and toys. Consider the following examples of data the store may wish to obtain or capture from the customer or the vendor:

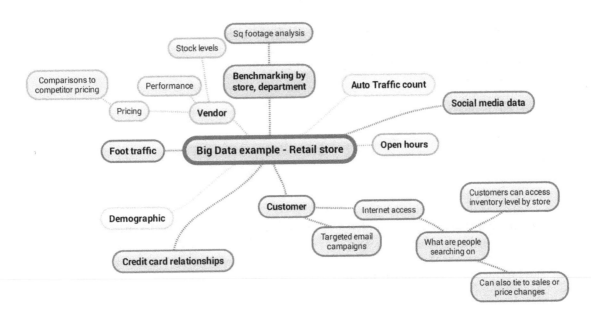

1. Customer: The organization's customer interacts in a variety of ways. An organization interested in Big Data will collect data from the customer through a variety of different methods and stages.
   a. *Internet access:* Assume that the customer is visiting the store via an Internet portal. The store would try to identify the customer through any of the following:
      i. A login identity
      ii. A home store
   b. *Key product and or sales data*
      i. What are people searching for?
         (1) Specific products, prices or price changes
         (2) Location of stores as well as inventory levels
         (3) What quantities do customers wish to buy?
         (4) Do they wish to pick up the item at the store?
         (5) What accessories or related items are being considered as well?
   c. *Targeted email campaigns:* Based on preferences shared by the customer, additional contacts can be made by email or text to induce a customer to make a purchase.
2. Vendor: The organization's vendor should also want significant access to data residing in the system.
   a. Performance: How fast is the product moving through inventory? Were the purchase requirements fulfilled correctly?
   b. Stock levels: What are the inventory levels? Also, and based on the lead times, when will it be necessary to replenish inventories level? If there are significant returns, what was the reason the products were returned?
   c. Pricing
      i. Comparisons to competitor pricing.
      ii. Is there any change in the mentor and movement based on the change in the retail price?

3. Demographic
   a. Where did the customer come from—or where is their home location?
   b. Would the customer be willing to complete a survey?
   c. Is the customer a member of a customer loyalty group?
4. Traffic count
   a. How many individuals entered through the front door?
   b. At what time did they enter through the front door?
5. Open hours
   a. Which hours of business accounted for the greatest sales?
   b. Which hours of business had the highest returns?
   c. Which hours of business had the most ancillary services sold such, as a small food shop (in-house fast food station?)
6. Credit card relationships
   a. How did people pay for the transaction?
      i. Cash
      ii. Check
      iii. Credit card
         (1) Affiliated
         (2) Type of card
         (3) Was the card rejected?
7. Benchmarking by store, department. Each of the sales transactions can be summarized by department or section within the store.
   a. Square footage analysis
   b. Sales relation to specific departments' weekly marketing brochures, emails, and the like
8. Social media information
   a. Did the user post a comment regarding any of the products or services?
   b. Did the user attempt to access online coupons for the product?
   c. Did the user review a secondary store if their home store was out of the inventory?

Practice Questions

1. Discuss the historical evolution of Big Data based on the interrelationships of recordkeeping, accounting, calculating machines, and Big Data?

2. Describe the sources of Big Data.

3. What are the four Vs?

4. List any three of the Big Data sources or uses of structured or unstructured data for a small retail business.

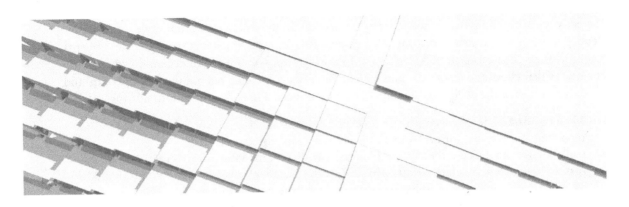

Chapter 3

WHAT ARE THE TRENDS IN BIG DATA?

LEARNING OBJECTIVES

After completing this chapter, you should be able to do the following:

- Distinguish between different Big Data trends.
- Identify how organizations are using Big Data and what their views are of Big Data going forward.

INTRODUCTION

What are the trends in Big Data? How are corporations reacting and planning to use Big Data in the coming years? An organization could gain a significant competitive advantage if it knows how to access and use Big Data. The trends in this chapter should be contrasted with your organization's Big Data approach and used as benchmarks in the company's strategic planning sessions.

TOP BIG DATA AND ANALYTICS TRENDS FOR 2017

Let's consider some of the trends impacting 2017 and the future. We will then consider trends that were highlighted in the previous edition of the course.

The activity surrounding Big Data continues to increase. In the following sections, we will attempt to identify some of the current trends for 2017, as well as recognize trends that were prevalent over the last couple of years. Professionals will identify the following as possibilities to understand and exploit. Businesses that choose to ignore the potential of Big Data risk falling behind their competitors and possibly not having the ability to catch up. Tableau produced a list of significant trends for 2017:[1]

1. Modern business intelligence (BI) becomes the new normal as it moves away from IT-centric reporting and is a tool for everyone in the organization, not just IT.
2. Collaborative analytics, rather than traditional one-directional information creation and dissemination, will generate new insights. Organizations, departments, and individuals will work together and create joint meaning from formerly disparate data sources.
3. Data of all shapes, sizes, and forms will be explored. The data environment will not be limited to spreadsheets and individual datasets, but will include a variety of data types from structured, semi-structured, and unstructured data.
4. Non-analysts will become involved in data preparation as the move to self-service data occurs. Deriving meaning from data will become a component of many jobs (not just restricted to accounting, engineering, or IT.) Non-analysts will be able to access, manipulate, analyze, and report on Big Data.
5. Analytics will be available to people at all levels of the organization. It will most likely become hidden in plain sight. Just as e-mail is a regular tool of business, Big Data and analytics will not be thought of as separate functions.
6. IT moves from producer to enabler. IT will develop systems that allow non-analysts to access information without requiring a completely new skill.
7. Data analysis becomes more intuitive with drag-and-drop applications rather than scripting or pivot tables. Analytics will be easier to use and therefore more readily adopted by non-analysts.
8. Transition to the cloud accelerates. The migration to the cloud will continue alleviating much of the maintenance formerly required for infrastructure and software.
9. Advanced analytics will move to the user ranks. Non-analysts will not only be able to access information but will be able to perform more complex analytics.

Trends From 2016

1. Smart machines—Computers, sensors, and the like are being created to set up data from Big Data sources, interpret that data, and take action on that data.
   a. Automating and removing human control—The processes are such that software is automating the identification, harvesting, analysis, and action phases so that human monitoring and intervention will not be necessary.
   b. Augmenting decision support or wearable technology—Big Data tools will supplement existing decision support and wearable technology. Consider how pharmacists could improve quality control (and patient safety) by ensuring that the meds they supply have no harmful interactions. It would also be possible to integrate physician records with pharmacy databases and compare to national benchmarks to ensure better efficacy and patient welfare. Another simple example is the wearable Fitbit device, which has an electronic signal that measures whether daily milestones have been achieved. When the milestone is reached, the Fitbit buzzes, and users know that they have reached a critical metric to support overall health or well-being.

---

[1] Ajenstat, Francois. "10 Business Intelligence Trends We Expect to See in 2017." *Tableau*, December 12, 2016. https://www.tableau.com/about/blog/2016/12/top-10-bi-trends-2017-63208. Accessed 3/29/17

2. Customer digital assistants—Big Data allows quicker recognition of related data that could improve the respective transaction processing.
   a. Systems that allow facial recognition and voice identification can be used to identify customers, employees, vendors, criminals, and so on. Emotion detection and natural language processing can reveal situations that can be detrimental or positive. Any opportunity to avert an unwanted situation would be welcomed by all parties. Also, positive instances can be recognized that showcase excellent customer or stakeholder interaction.
3. Machines authoring content—Big Data applications have resulted in computers venturing into journalistic areas. Computers are capable of writing:
   a. Reports, white papers, press releases, articles and the like.
   b. Robot writers are currently preparing thousands of fantasy football newsletter stories.
   c. Expect advances in business content assistants such as Siri and Cortana. As computers become more advanced, personal software assistants will be able to integrate with Big Data analysis to enhance data query and processing instructions.
4. Robo Management
   a. For repetitive positions, it is foreseeable that management will be robots. If the repetitive position can be benchmarked, a computer will be able to analyze, point out deviations from expectations and provide training and assistance to improve performance. This ability will be enhanced by computers that have self-learning capabilities.
5. Internet of Anything—The concept of Big Data included the "Internet of Things" (IoT), which means sensors and streaming data. This idea will morph into the "Internet of Anything." Disparate information generators will be accessed, aggregated and interpreted to produce new understanding.
   a. The expectation from management will be to draw value from everything.
   b. Examples of data that could be integrated into key metrics and financial information are oil rigs, satellites, weather buoys, GPS, and so on.
   c. Unfortunately, the tools are not as robust as required, so additional development is expected to integrate all different levels of Big Data sources.
6. Big Data simplification—Even though Big Data discussion has been around for over 5 years, it has required a certain degree of expertise.
   a. All users of Big Data are looking forward to simplification of the tools for access, integration, and analysis to create greater value.
   b. Security—As seen by recent breaches involving Guccifer, Edward Snowden, and Julian Assange, companies have an enormous risk in the data maintained in their systems. The advancements in Big Data will only increase the potential exposure. Expect organizations in the future to improve their processes and systems to be in compliance with laws and regulations. Companies will also define how they will use Big Data, including information that has been captured or created based on customer or stakeholder information.
7. In 2016, Big Data will be used to create more customized applications for end users. Application developers will use data and analytics to create personalized, engaging experiences. The applications will try to unite related data across industries such as sports, energy, social well-being, and music. As an example, users will be able to select music based on personal preferences, such as instruments and tempo.
   a. As part of the user-generated data discovery—friendlier end-user tools will be made available to allow less sophisticated users to participate in Big Data analysis. The number of software tools such as Tableau, Qlikview, and Excel BI will increase. This effort will become known as self-service data analytics
8. Hadoop will allow mission critical applications thatweren't previously available. Hadoop is a tool that enables access to disparate databases. Due to increased usage and demands, expect to see Hadoop usage grow and become applied to central company applications.
9. The growth of Big Data will also result in the personalization of applications for the end user. Early in the development of the Internet, end users could create their home portal with critical data that they were interested in, such as weather, news, and stock prices. This new trend will allow end users

to access, mine and predict Big Data outcomes just as if they were asking for the weather or the news.

10. Apache Spark is moving from a component of the Hadoop software to the Big Data platform of choice.

11. Although the original vision of Big Data was to house it internally, major Big Data companies such as Google, Amazon, and others are integrating Big Data, the cloud, and IoT. Just as they were key players in migrating to the cloud, they are making the same inroads with organizations moving their Big Data efforts from internal to the cloud.

12. Executive teams will embrace algorithms as tools to increase or generate value. The strategic objectives will include efforts to identify the value-adding algorithms.

13. There is a need to act quickly to access, analyze, decide and act before Big Data loses value and the company loses competitive advantage. At a bare minimum, companies in 2016 must address Big Data during their strategic planning sessions.

14. Big Data will allow improved access to image recognition and natural language understanding. Also, it should provide the potential to increase deeper learning and understanding than what is currently achieved.

    a. The expansion of Big Data capabilities will provide more context around data such as demographics and location.

15. Big Data will migrate away from simple data dumps to improved access and mining of existing databases.

16. As Big Data evolves, professionals will be required to understand and manipulate data to their advantage. The role of data scientist will be incorporated into many existing job descriptions.

17. Machine learning will increase and replace traditional manual trial and error that humans currently attempt.

    a. Expect Big Data devices to collect, analyze, and store data without human intervention. For those attendees who love movies, consider the examples of Danny DeVito's computer to search out breakup candidates in *Other People's Money*, or the psychopathic computer HAL in the movie *2001: A Space Odyssey*.

18. There is a good chance that the term "Big Data" may go by the wayside and descriptions will be focused on the specific segments of collecting, storing, mining, algorithms, and so on.

19. According to the Bureau of Labor Statistics, there is a shortage of skilled data scientists for the next several years.

20. MPP (multi-parallel processing), which was touted as being an in-house system, will most likely move to the cloud.

The trends in the following sections were highlighted in the first edition of this course, released in the summer of 2015. The trends were identified via surveys and studies performed by the following leading consulting firms:

- Gartner & Co.
- Accenture
- NewVantage Partners

BIG DATA SURVEY

Gartner & Co. is a leading consulting company specializing in information technology.

Gartner believes the rapidly evolving modern BI and analytics market is being influenced by the following seven dynamics:

1. Modern BI tools that support greater accessibility, agility, and analytical insight at the enterprise level will dominate new purchases.
2. The emergence of smart data discovery capabilities, machine learning, and automation of the entire analytics workflow will drive a new flurry of buying by established vendors because of their potential value to reduce time to insights from advanced analytics and deliver those insights to a broader set of people across the enterprise.
3. There will be a larger investment in data preparation of complex datasets as business users want to analyze increasingly large, diverse, and complex combinations of data sources and data models, faster than ever before.
4. The ability to embed and extend analytics content will be a key enabler of more pervasive adoption of and ability to gain value from analytics.
5. Organizations will increasingly leverage streaming data generated by devices, sensors, and people to make faster decisions.
6. Cloud deployments of BI and analytics platforms have the potential to reduce the cost of ownership and speed time to deployment. Gartner expects that, by 2020, the majority of new licensing buying is likely to be for cloud deployments.
7. The availability of an active marketplace where buyers and sellers converge to exchange analytic applications, aggregated data sources, custom visualizations, and algorithms is likely to generate increased interest in the BI and analytics space and fuel its future growth.

Organizations will benefit from the many new and innovative vendors continuing to emerge.[2]

In other studies, Gartner also pointed out the following:

Increased Use of Drones

Production of drones for personal and commercial use is growing rapidly, with global market revenue expected to increase 34 percent to reach more than $6 billion in 2017 and grow to more than $11.2 billion by 2020, according to a new forecast from Gartner, Inc. Almost three million drones will be produced in 2017, 39 percent more than in 2016.

The market for commercial drones is much smaller than the consumer market, with a significantly higher average selling price in comparison with personal drones. With more countries solidifying their drone regulations, the market is beginning to stabilize, and companies are now buying drones to test and deploy in nearly every industry. Commercial drones normally have a higher payload, longer flight times, and redundant sensors and flight controllers to make them safer. They are more specialized to a function, such as mapping, delivery, or industrial inspection, so prices vary according to these requirements.[3]

---

[2] www.gartner.com/ newsroom/ id/ 3612617, accessed 3/ 29/ 17
[3] www.gartner.com/ newsroom/ id/ 3602317, accessed 3/ 29/ 17

Gartner, Inc., forecasts that 8.4 billion connected things will be in use worldwide in 2017, up 31 percent from 2016, and will reach 20.4 billion by 2020. Total spending on endpoints and services will reach almost $2 trillion in 2017.

Regionally, Greater China, North America, and Western Europe are driving the use of connected things and the three regions together will represent 67 percent of the overall IoT installed base in 2017.

The consumer segment is the largest user of connected things, with 5.2 billion units in 2017, which represents 63 percent of the overall number of applications in use. Businesses are on pace to employ 3.1 billion connected things in 2017.[4]

KNOWLEDGE CHECK

1. Gartner forecasts that how many connected things will be in use by 2017?

    a. 4.4 billion.
    b. 6.8 billion.
    c. 8.4 billion.
    d. 9.6 billion

ACCENTURE TRENDS AND SURVEYS

In March of 2017, Accenture conducted a study that concluded that **nearly half (48 percent) of CFOs believe digital technologies will fundamentally change everything finance does.**[5]

Some of their other findings include the following:

- Eight in 10 CFOs are seeing measurable return on investment (ROI) from digital finance investments.
- One in four companies realize greater than expected returns from digital, and 82 percent are seeing measurable business ROI from digital finance investments. In addition, finance organizations reported the following:
    - 86 percent can better manage risk.
    - 67 percent have improved their forecast accuracy.
    - 66 percent report better decision making.
    - 61 percent say finance teams are dedicating more time to high-value work.[6]
- Today's CFOs are embracing digital more than ever. It is much more than social, mobile and analytics. CFOs are increasingly relying on digital for

---

[4] www.gartner.com/ newsroom/ id/ 3598917, accessed 3/ 29/ 17

[5] https:/ / accntu.re/ 2m9H0Ca, accessed 3/ 29/ 17

[6] https:/ / newsroom.accenture.com/ news/ nearly-half-of-chief-financial-officers-believe-digital-technologies-will-fundamentally-change-everything-finance-does-according-to-accenture-strategy.htm Accesses 3/ 29/ 17

- security threat intelligence,
- blockchain, and
- artificial intelligence.
- Digital is currently delivering improvement in professional staff productivity and could soon make monthly, and quarterly, management reports a relic of a bygone time.
- About one-third of all digital technologies have delivered transformational benefits to firms with cycle time reduction (37 percent) and finance staff productivity improvement (36 percent) being the top benefits.
- The study also highlighted a few barriers:
  - The level of investment required for digital technologies (18 percent)
  - Hiring talent that has the required skills to implement and operate the new technologies (16 percent)

In an earlier Accenture study entitled, "Big Success with Big Data," the consulting firm listed the following five major findings:

1. Big Data is taking off. Users who have completed a Big Data project are satisfied with the results.
2. Bigger companies are getting more from Big Data. Companies are achieving a more significant payback.
3. Big Data demands broad learning. Organizations will have to invest in training tools.
4. Expert outside help will be needed. It is difficult to find skilled in-house talent.
5. Big Data is disruptive but potentially transformational.

Illustration 3-1

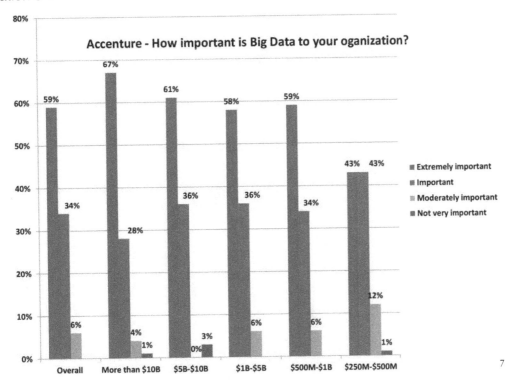

---

[7] Ibid.

Illustration 3-2

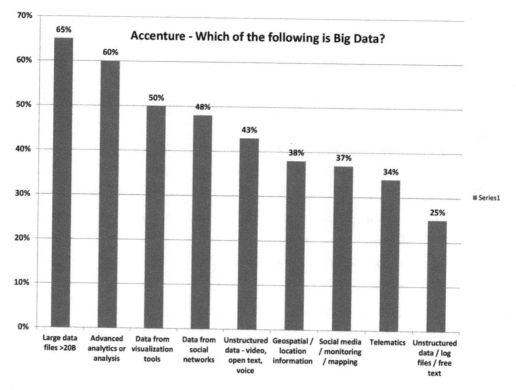

Accenture - Which of the following is Big Data?

Illustration 3-3

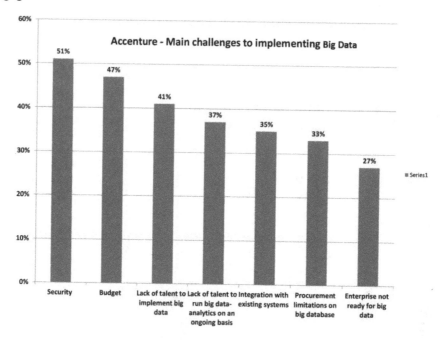

Accenture - Main challenges to implementing Big Data

Illustration 3-4

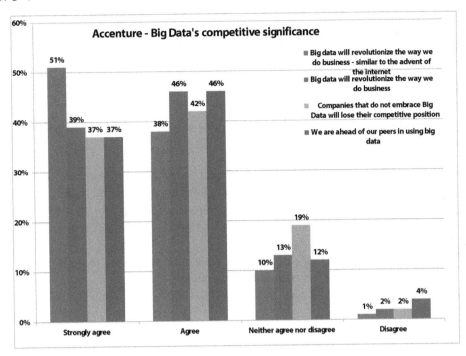

KNOWLEDGE CHECK

2. Users who have completed a Big Data project are _____ with the results.

    a. Ambivalent.
    b. Dissatisfied.
    c. Satisfied.
    d. Ecstatic.

3. According to Accenture, what is the most widely accepted characteristic of Big Data?

    a. Advanced analytics.
    b. File sizes > 20TB.
    c. Data from social networks.
    d. Data from machines.

4. What percentage of respondents strongly agree that companies will lose competitive position if they do not embrace Big Data?

    a. 51 percent.
    b. 39 percent.
    c. 37 percent.
    d. 62 percent.

NEWVANTAGE PARTNERS 5TH ANNUAL BIG DATA EXECUTIVE SURVEY[8]

According to NewVantage Partners 5th annual Big Data Executive Survey, 48.4 percent of corporate executives who were surveyed indicated that their firm has achieved "measurable results" from their Big Data investments. Further, a remarkable 80.7 percent of executives now characterize their Big Data efforts as having been successful.

The survey highlights the challenges that major corporations still face as they seek to become more data-driven organizations:

- 85.5 percent of executives report that their organization has taken steps to create a data-driven culture, but only 37.7 percent report that these efforts have been successful to date.
- 52.5 percent of executives report that organizational impediments, including lack of organizational alignment, business or technology resistance, and lack of middle management adoption are factors limiting the success of Big Data efforts.
- 60.7 percent of executives report that their firm has developed an enterprise Big Data strategy, but 18 percent report that their firm lacks "a coherent data strategy."
- 95 percent of executives report that their organization has undertaken a Big Data initiative within the past five years.
- The survey shows a range of Big Data initiatives:
  - Efforts to decrease expenses through operational cost efficiencies have proven to be successful (49.2 percent) for many firms.
  - Only 27.9 percent of respondents believe they have achieved a data-driven culture.
  - New avenues for innovation and disruption have had the highest success rate—64.5 percent started, 44.3 percent reporting results, 68.7 percent success rate.

KNOWLEDGE CHECK

5. According to the NewVantage Partners survey, approximately what percentage of respondents reported success with Big Data efforts to achieve cost efficiencies by reducing expenses?

    a. 10 percent.
    b. 30 percent.
    c. 50 percent.
    d. 70 percent.

---

[8] Executives Report Measurable Results From Big Data, But…, https://www.forbes.com/sites/ciocentral /2017/01/10/executives-report-measurable- Accessed 3/29/17

CSC Study—Big Data and Analytics

CSC (Computer Sciences Corporation) prepared a study entitled "Big Data & Analytics—From Sensory Overload to Predictable Outcomes." [9] The survey highlights CFO and CIO expectations from Big Data and how to gain a competitive advantage by mastering Big Data.

The major points of the survey were the following:

1. Data are a competitive tool for any organization. However, it must be the correct data, properly managed and arranged, and must come from a wide range of sources.
2. Data must be transformed into actionable business insights.
3. Eager enthusiasts use Big Data for historical perspectives.
4. Half of those surveyed believed that Big Data could have as much of an impact on their organization as the World Wide Web did.
5. The majority of CFOs say that the quality of data and the speed at which it is delivered is adequate.
6. Most CFOs see Big Data as a cost.
7. To successfully take advantage of Big Data, business and information technology development must work together.
8. More than half of the respondents employed data scientists, mathematicians, or pattern trackers.
9. There must be one individual who is charged with the responsibility of bringing together large amounts of data successfully from a variety of sources as part of the strategic decision making for the organization.

---

[9] "Big Data Analytics—From Sensory Overload to Predictable Outcomes," CSC, accessed 3/29/17, https://assets1.csc.com/big_data/downloads/8099_14_Big_Data_Overview.pdf

Practice Questions

1. In which industries does Tableau believe that Big Data will create more customized applications?

2. What does Accenture conclude about internal talent for Big Data projects?

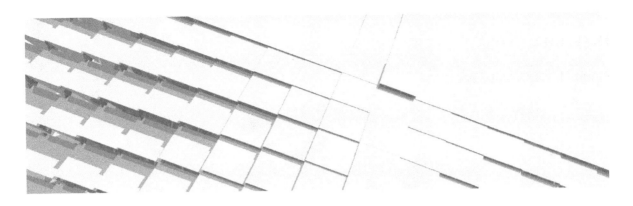

Chapter 4

WHAT ARE THE STRATEGY AND BUSINESS APPLICATIONS OF BIG DATA?

LEARNING OBJECTIVES

After completing this chapter, you should be able to do the following:

- Distinguish the root reason for a Big Data strategy.
- Recall the goals of Big Data.
- Identify the strategic implications of Big Data.

INTRODUCTION

Figure 4-1: Big Data Goals

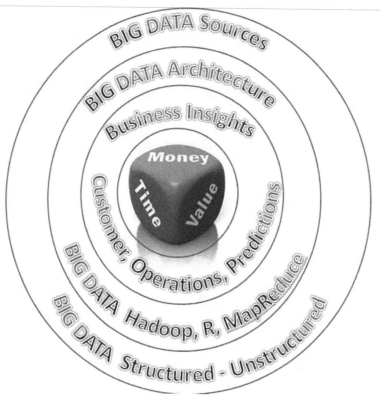

All business endeavors must increase value for shareholders or stakeholders. In this chapter, we're going to consider the strategic implications of Big Data to an organization. What are the goals an organization should have in regards to Big Data? What type of strategies should be created to achieve the goals? How does an organization begin the journey of implementing Big Data? The first step for all these questions is to determine the overall objective of the organization and how Big Data will be used to help achieve that objective.

For-profit organizations focus on increasing enterprise value as their main objective or purpose. The main objective or purpose for not-for-profits must be to enhance the lives, services, and opportunities for the customers or stakeholders. In figure 4-1, notice that the center purpose is money, time, or value.

The first circle outside money, time, or value represents business insights. For the organization to enhance the enterprise or stakeholder's value, it must consider business insights that affect the customer, operations, or predictions as to future results. When acted upon, the insights should yield an increase in the organization's value.

The second circle represents Big Data architecture. The architecture indicates that for the organization to achieve business insights, it will most likely be required to make an investment in Big Data architecture. Big Data architecture has a myriad of hardware, software, and consultant options. It also involves software programs such as Hadoop, R, and MapReduce. It is safe to assume that without making an investment in the Big Data architecture, it will be very difficult to generate business insights relating to Big Data that will yield increased value.

The final circle represents Big Data sources. This level encompasses all of the structured and unstructured sources of Big Data that have been covered previously. If an organization is unwilling or incapable of accessing and analyzing Big Data sources, the organization will not be able to generate insights that will lead to increased enterprise or stakeholder value.

KNOWLEDGE CHECK

1. Big Data requires that all business endeavors add as their root objective the goal of

    a. Increasing value for shareholders or stakeholders.
    b. Increasing scalable architecture.
    c. Increasing Big Data capacity.
    d. Data aggregation.

GOALS OF BIG DATA

The overarching goal of Big Data analytics is to inform businesses. By analyzing data and trends, businesses can gain valuable insights that can be applied in nearly every area of operations. Some specific ways that Big Data can contribute to achieving the goal of informing businesses include the following:

- Monetize data or interpret data to realize competitive advantage which can be monetized.
- Analyze operational effectiveness—machine sensors, product failures, and traffic patterns.
- Create a reliable, scalable, and capable infrastructure that aids the data gathering, analysis, and inferences.
- Access and use internal and external data that are structured, unstructured, and streaming.
- Predict business, social, political, economic, technological, and environmental trends.
- Take action based on prescribed scenarios.

BUSINESS INSIGHTS ASSOCIATED WITH BIG DATA

The following list attempts to convey the wide variety of applications of Big Data. Many of the data components relate to multiple industries.

1. *Customer analytics.* As noted in a previous chapter, one of the main sources of Big Data comes from transactions. This kind of information from customers can be used to gain insights into many aspects of customer behavior, including the following:
    - Dropping product or service
    - Analyzing customer behavior while on company website
    - Monitoring customer usage of products to detect manufacturing or design problems
    - Identifying high-value customers
    - Identifying cross-selling opportunities as well as up-selling opportunities
    - Determining which customers not to engage

- Identifying, targeting, and retaining customers
- Combining clickstream data with transactional data to improve customer profile
- Limiting product offerings to those that interest the customer
- Determining any aspect of customer behavior or product preference
- Identifying customer segmentation
- Recording and analyzing customer service and support issues
- Engaging brand advocates and changing the perception of brand antagonists
- Empowering customers to sell your products
- Enabling customers to locate items more quickly
- Improving loyalty or net to promote are scores
- Analyzing smartphone or mobile data—called detail record processing, social analysis, churn prediction, GEO mapping
- Analyzing point of sale data
- Creating forums—crowd creativity, crowd solutions

2. *Manufacturing.* Manufacturers now have access to real-time data from a variety of process activities that allow them to gain insight into many factors, including the following:
   - Tracking of product quality or defects
   - Supply chain management and planning
   - Optimizing machines
   - Engineering Analytics
   - Predictive maintenance
   - Process and quality analysis
   - Warranty claim potential (based on social media comments or complaints)
   - Enterprise resource planning—operations, service delivery, supply chain management, and automation of routine decisions
   - Continuous improvement to processes and procedures

3. *Research and development.* Recently, the federal government recognized the potential value that lies in Big Data for research and development. A new initiative was launched that intends to extract knowledge from collections of digital data to help solve challenges on a national level. On a business level, Big Data can help with the following:
   - Monitoring product quality
   - Identifying customer needs for potential new products
   - Soliciting input from customers regarding products
   - Improving products based on call center data

4. *Distribution.* As warehouses and distribution centers become increasingly high-tech, they now generate information that can be used to monitor and track labor, inventory, and equipment, including the following:
   - Monitoring product shipments
   - Identifying variances in logistic costs
   - Determining inventories levels
   - Using location data like GPS
   - Using Radio-frequency identification
   - Using distribution optimization

5. *Logistics.* "Information of Things" is a huge new source of data in logistics. It can be used to track goods and provide insight into the following:
   - Demand forecasting
   - Supply chain analytics

- Tracking
- Delivery forecasting
- Travel industry—searchers, pricing, bundling (air, hotel, car, ship, entertainment)

6. *Marketing.* Marketing departments are no stranger to using data to determine customers' habits. With great access to data, they can apply their insights to the following:
   - Determining marketing campaign effectiveness
   - Determining channel effectiveness
   - Monitoring and improving customer experience
   - Tailoring marketing campaigns based on location and demographic data
   - Providing advertising and public relations campaigns—demand signaling, targeted advertising, sentiment analysis, customer acquisition, promotions, and other advertising mediums
   - Offering brand sentiment analysis
   - Providing product placement optimization
   - Providing response modeling
   - Providing retention modeling
   - Providing market-based analysis
   - Providing net promoter scores
   - Providing customer segmentation

7. *Predictions.* Big Data may enable predictions to be made in areas other than business. Some of these include the following:
   - Crimes, threat analysis
   - Weather
   - Investments
   - Mineral location
   - Astrophysics
   - Health
   - Relationships

8. *Operations analysis.* Operations analysis leverages information from machine sensors to improve operations in many ways, including the following:
   - More accurate and timely decision making
   - Deviation analysis of logs and operational data
   - Facility layout—either in manufacturing or retail
   - Supply chain optimization
   - Dynamic pricing

9. *Human Resources.* Some retail companies use wearable technology to track their employees' communications and movements within stores. Although that's an extreme example of using Big Data for human resources, many companies can use information about their employees to do some of the following:
   - Identify employees at risk to leave company
   - Monitor recruitment activities
   - Identify recruits external candidates
   - Résumé data
   - Employee search
   - Employee future team

10. *Accounting.* We will discuss some of the following applications in other chapters of this course:
    - Measuring risk
      - Credit risk

- Market risk
- Operational risk
- Budgeting, forecasting, planning
- Fraud detection
  - Detecting multiparty fraud
  - Real-time fraud prevention
- Algorithmic trading
- Customer analysis
- Duplicate payments
- Pricing, business intelligence, and data mining

11. *Competition*
- Tracking competitors' prices
- Tracking competitors' sales
- Tracking competitors' marketing initiatives
- Mapping out the competitive landscape

12. *Media and telecommunications*. Network optimization, customer scoring, sure and prevention, fraud prevention

13. *Energy*. Smart grid analysis, exploration, operational modeling, power line sensors

14. *Healthcare and life sciences*. Bioinformatics, pharmaceutical research, clinical outcomes research, pharmacogenomics, neonatal, ICU monitoring, epidemic early warning system, remote healthcare monitoring, likely return to the hospital.
- Drug discovery
- Health cures
- Health diagnosis

15. *Government*
- Regulatory compliance
- Threat analysis
- Law enforcement, defense, and cyber security (for example, real-time surveillance, situational awareness, cyber security detection, license plate tracking, GPS tracking)
- Natural systems—wildfire management, water management, wildlife management
- Transportation—intelligent traffic management
- Tax avoidance, Social Security fraud, money laundering, terrorist detection, communication surveillance and monitoring, market governance, weapons systems and counterterrorism, econometrics, health informatics

16. *Unstructured data*. Related to many of the preceding sections
- Sensor data—automotive, appliance, machine, temperature, security, vending machine
- Social networking—sentiment data from user-generated comments on ratings, reviews, and blogs
- Text messaging SMS Software—application logs
- Internet search—text and documents, mining
- Digital images and videos
- Voice data
- Web—web analytics, social media analytics, multivariate testing (Multivariate testing is a technique for testing a hypothesis in which multiple variables are modified. The goal of multivariate testing is to determine which combination of variations performs the best out of all of the possible combinations. Websites and mobile apps are made of combinations of changeable elements.)[1]

---

[1] "What Is Multivariate Testing?" *Optipedia*, Accessed 3/ 30/ 17, www.optimizely.com/ resources/ multivariate-testing/

- Other—text analytics, business process analytics
- Clickstream—a virtual trail that a user leaves behind while surfing the Internet. A clickstream is a record of a user's activity on the Internet, including every website and every page of every website that the user visits, how long the user was on a page or site, in what order the pages were visited, any newsgroups that the user participates in, and even the email addresses of mail that the user sends and receives. Both Internet service providers and individual websites are capable of tracking a user's clickstream.[2]

17. *Stock market analysis.* For example, the impact of weather on security prices or analysis of market data latencies

KNOWLEDGE CHECKS

2. Which of the following was not mentioned as a Big Data insight as it relates to research and development?

   a. Monitoring product quality.
   b. Identifying customer needs.
   c. Creating third- and fourth-generation products.
   d. Soliciting input from customers.

Big Data Architecture

Figure 4-2

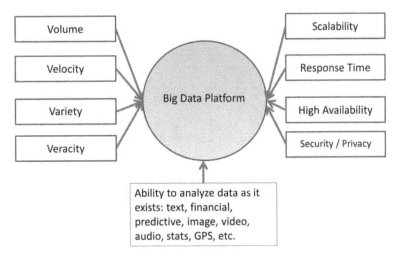

Source: Adapted from information found on bigdataandanalysis.blogspot.com/

In order to provide all of the insights needed for businesses, a Big Data platform needs to accomplish many goals. Big Data architecture must be designed so that data are analyzed in the natural environment

---

[2] "Clickstream," *Webopedia*, Accessed 3/ 30/ 17, webopedia.com

as opposed to recreating data in voluminous data tables. The architecture must allow for reading and accessing a variety of sources such as email, financial, audio, images, GPS, and the like. The architecture should be created to accomplish the four Vs—volume, velocity, variety, and veracity—as described in chapter 2. The architecture must also be economically scalable, have an adequate response time, have multiple hardware options (due to hardware failures), and have built-in security to prevent unauthorized access to confidential detailed data.

STRATEGIC IMPLICATIONS OF BIG DATA—CHALLENGES

To pursue Big Data as a tool for the organization, there are some key strategic issues that first must be addressed. If the strategic issues are overlooked at the beginning of the process, it may be difficult to implement Big Data successfully. The following list can be used as a starting point to think about implementing a Big Data platform:

- Strategic challenges
  - Establishing suitability for purpose
  - Providing an overall system architectural plan
- Technological challenges
  - Gaining access to data
  - Gaining access to the associated methodology and metadata
  - Establishing provenance and lineage of data sets
  - Establishing data set quality with respect to a city (accuracy, fidelity), uncertainty, error, bias, reliability, and calibration
  - Addressing security concerns
  - Technological feasibility
  - Existing data warehouse architecture
  - Immature new systems or reliability of selected data
  - Lack of metadata and schema for the Big Data
  - Lack of tooling
  - Availability of enterprise-ready products and tools
  - High latency (Hadoop)
  - Running inside the cluster
- Resource or capacity challenges
  - Ability to implement a wide-scale Big Data initiative
  - Consolidation of disparate data
  - Quality and cost of collecting data
  - Budget constraints
  - Cost too high
- Staff challenges
  - Experiment and trial testing big analytics
  - Integrity of network transmission
  - Poor data quality
  - Ability to deal with real-time data
- Project management challenges
  - Reliance on multiple consultants that may not work in harmony
  - Starting with the right project
- Change management challenges

- Institutional change management
- Ensuring inter-jurisdictional collaboration and common standards
- Different department systems that inhibit collection and organization of Big Data
- Acquiring technically competent staff
- Steep technical learning curve
- Hiring qualified people
- Barriers between departments that are cultural and nature
- Data that are not accepted or believed
- Data ownership especially as it tries to organization culture
- Lack of business sponsorship
- Lack of belief in a business case
- Partnership challenges
  - Forming strategic alliances with Big Data producers
- Legal and regulatory issues

Table 4-1

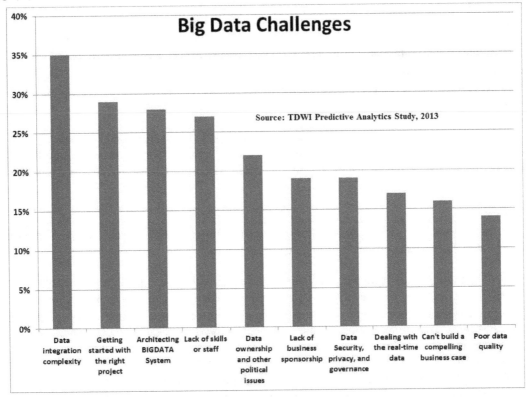

Source: Adapted from www.business2community.com/big-data/drive-real-time-revenue-world-big-data-01109279

KNOWLEDGE CHECK

3. According to TDWI, what is the biggest challenge for Big Data?

   a. Lack of business sponsorship.
   b. Lack of skills for IT staff.
   c. Data integration complexity.
   d. Poor data quality.

DANGERS OF WRONG DATA

In addition to the strategic challenges of using Big Data, there is also a significant potential that an organization might use Big Data incorrectly. There are many situations which could jeopardize the integrity of the decision-making process if an organization uses Big Data without fully understanding statistical pitfalls. Any issues with small amounts of data will be magnified in larger quantities. Sample error or bias could create data that is not representative of the situation, a common inaccuracy found in polling. False assumptions could be the collection of data from the very beginning. For example, a company may assume that a variable is a strong predictor of customer retention, but in reality, that variable is only correlated to retention.

There's a major danger that organizations become entranced with aggregating vast amounts of data only to draw improper conclusions regarding that data. This is especially important for manufacturing environments which may make crucial production decisions based on prescriptive analytics.

Wrong data

Let us consider an example that Ari Zoldan wrote about in *Wired* magazine, which discussed drawing conclusions from Twitter data collected during Hurricane Sandy.[3]

> In an intriguing study from Rutgers University, scientists set out to understand people's decision-making related to Hurricane Sandy. From October 27th to November 1st, over 20 million tweets were recorded that pertained to the super storm. Tweets concerning preparedness peaked the night before, and tweets about partying peaked after the storm subsided.
>
> The majority of the tweets originated from Manhattan, largely because of the high concentration of smartphone and Twitter usage. Due to the high concentration of power outages, and diminishing cell phone batteries, very few tweets were made from the hardest hit areas, such as Seaside Heights and Midland Beach. From the data, one could infer that the Manhattan borough bared the brunt of the storm; however, we know that wasn't the case. There was actually a lot going on in those outlying areas. Given the way the data was presented, there was a huge data gap from communities unrepresented in the Twittersphere.

---

[3] Ari Zoldan, "More Data, More Problems: Is Big Data Always Right?" Wired, accessed March 17, 2016, www.wired.com/ 2013/ 05/ more-data-more-problems-is-big-data-always-right/

This example illustrates several points. First, it refutes the myth that more data will create greater insights. It demonstrates the importance of not being overly influenced by volumes of data or statistics. As you look at data, be objective, critical, and independent of any outcome.

Statistics does not mean facts. Big Data may appear to be factual when it is just more volume. When it is raw, Big Data is large and unorganized, and organizing data for analysis is difficult.

You should also be wary of biases and missing context. Confirmation bias is the phenomenon that people search the data to confirm their preexisting viewpoint. Also, when data conflict with underlying assumptions, there is a tendency to ignore it. Just because the data can be charted or analyzed by an algorithm, it does not mean the interpretation is valid. Faster and more powerful systems mean that we can also make the wrong interpretation and prescription faster than ever.

When evaluating data, keep the following three cautions in mind:

1. People tend to find what they seek. More data and speed do not necessarily mean that the results will be improved.
2. There are two types of data—quantitative and qualitative. Qualitative analysis is necessary to explain the quantitative analysis. Consider the announcement of public earnings reports. The numbers are announced. Then they are put into context by explaining or "verbally" adjusting earnings to present in the best light.
3. Remember that the context of data is very important. Consider how global warming has been interpreted, reinterpreted, and reinterpreted again. For every data set, it is important to understand the analyst's bias, such as data presented, data modified, and data excluded. For example, the first quarter gross domestic product in 2015 did not come in as high as hoped. The first quarter has been lower than expected each of the past couple of years. Analysts originally credited this performance to harsh winters. Unfortunately, the weather still didn't account for all of the disappointing results, so analysts stated that there was a "first quarter residual seasonality" and soft readings in other variables. It should be noted that the economists of the Federal Reserve did not find significant statistical evidence for such distortions on the aggregate GDP.[4]

FIVE IT BIG DATA MISTAKES

How big is the problem of Big Data for the information technology manager? According to Infochimps:

> 55% of Big Data projects don't get completed, and many others fall short of their objectives.

> Though there may be many reasons for this, undoubtedly one of the biggest factors is a lack of communication between top managers, who provide the overall project vision, and those charged with implementing it. Far too frequently the opinions of the IT staff doing the heavy lifting necessary to develop a Big Data project are taken as an afterthought and consequently considered only when projects veer off-course.[5]

---

[4] "Residual Seasonality in GDP," FEDS Notes, Federal Reserve, accessed March 17, 2016, www.federalreserve.gov/ econresdata/ notes/ feds-notes/ 2015/ residual-seasonality-in-gdp-20150514.html

[5] "Big Data: What Your IT Team Wants You to Know," Infochimps, accessed March 18, 2016, www.infochimps.com/ resources/ report-cios-big-data-what-your-it-team-wants-you-to-know-6/

According to that quote, almost half of Big Data projects are never finished. Of those remaining, a large subset will not add value to the organization or stakeholders. In addition to potential mistakes with data selection and processing, IT can add complications. Subramanian Iyer of Oracle wrote about the five Big Data mistakes that IT makes:[6]

1. Too much emphasis on the technology needed rather than the business need.
2. Many times IT management focuses on the wrong business cases assuming that the payback will be the same as others in the industry.
3. Management may launch multiple initiatives in parallel as part of a big bang approach to implementing Big Data. This approach may lessen the chances of success with Big Data projects.
4. Many times IT management does not complete a proper cost-benefit analysis to determine what the payback on the Big Data project will be.
5. Placing a Big Data application under the same process requirements (mechanism for authentication, access, data isolation, and management of environments) as compared to traditional applications may jeopardize the project.

KNOWLEDGE CHECK

4. Which of these is NOT a Big Data mistake?

    a. Using an iterative implementation strategy.
    b. Focusing on technology instead of the business need.
    c. Not executing a cost-benefit analysis.
    d. Executing multiple initiatives in parallel as part of a "big bang" approach or pilot implementations.

---

[6] Subramanian Iyer, "Five Big Data Mistakes," Oracle, accessed June 8, 2015, www.oracle.com/ us/ corporate/ profit/ big-ideas/ 031214-siyer-2166578.html.

Practice Questions

1. What is the root reason for developing Big Data?

2. What are some of the change management issues confronting Big Data implementations?

3. A cautionary tale of Big Data and tweets was related to Hurricane Sandy. What occurred with related tweets that, taken out of context, might produce a false conclusion?

Chapter 5

BIG DATA PLATFORMS AND OPERATING TOOLS

LEARNING OBJECTIVES

After completing this chapter, you should be able to do the following:

- Recognize which Big Data software tools are available for use.
- Identify the open-source software known as Hadoop.
- Recall the role of map reduce and R software.

INTRODUCTION

This chapter identifies a variety of Big Data platforms as well as the operating tools that can be used on those platforms. Chief among the tools is the operating system known as Hadoop. Hadoop is an open-source framework that many organizations have chosen to support their Big Data efforts. This chapter will concentrate on information technology terms that are necessary for accountants to have foundational understanding in Big Data applications.

BIG DATA CAPABILITIES

The first step in all Big Data is understanding what the organization hopes to achieve. There should be two discussions that occur.

First, the organization should conduct a strategic planning retreat. The main question that should be asked is: What is the long-term vision for the company as it relates to Big Data?

Next, the organization should conduct an information planning retreat. This discussion should focus on how the organization can achieve the strategy for the first step with existing resources (hardware, software, staff, and future budget).

Both of these conversations are necessary and should take place in two different planning meetings. One way to approach the needs of the organization is by examining some of the capabilities of Big Data and then determining if any of them complement the corporate or IT strategy.

Table 5-1

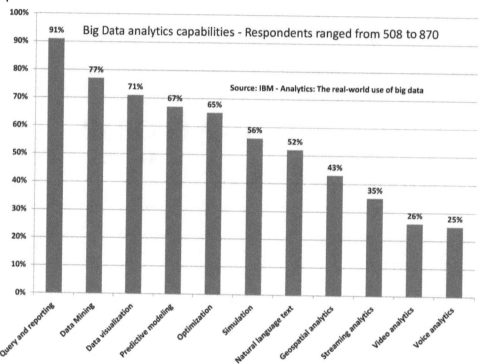

Source Adapted from "The Real-World Use of Big Data," IBM Institute for Business Value, accessed March 18, 2016, www-935.ibm.com/services/us/gbs/thoughtleadership/ibv-big-data-at-work.html

Data analytics (DA) is the study of analyzing raw information with the goal of achieving inferences about that data. DA is used as a part of numerous commercial ventures to help organizations make better business choices and to confirm or refute existing models or speculations. DA is different from "data mining" in that it includes an evaluation process that data mining does not necessarily have. Data mining involves searching large information sets to discover patterns and relationships. DA focuses on deducing an answer based on what the analyst knows.

Data analysis involves inspection, cleaning, revising, and modeling with the objective of finding valuable data, proposing conclusions, and supporting wise choices. Data analysis has different features and methodologies, with many techniques and applications of business, science, and sociology areas.

Data mining is a technique that focuses on modeling and discovery for predictive purposes. Business intelligence focuses on aggregating enterprise data. In statistical applications, there are descriptive statistics and the following main types of data analysis:

- Exploratory: Finds new characteristics in data.
- Confirmatory: Affirms or denies existing beliefs.
- Predictive: Concentrates on statistical models for forecasting purposes.
- Text: Extracts and classifies information from unstructured data (such as email) using statistical, structural, and linguistic techniques.

Predictive analytics focuses on predicting future results or patterns based on extracted data from existing data sets. It does not guarantee the results it only forecasts what might happen with some degree of reliability and incorporates "What-if" scenarios and risk or sensitivity analysis. Predictive analytics can include practices such as data mining, statistical modeling, and machine learning.

The following chart depicts the applications in business that are most aligned with predictive analytics.

Table 5-2

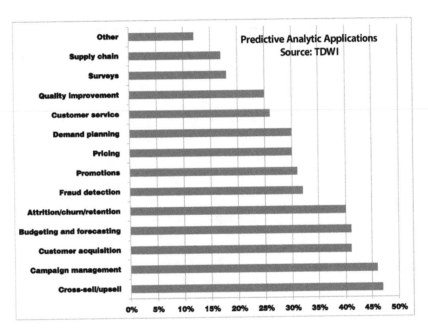

Source: Adapted from http://tdwi.org/articles/2007/05/10/predictive-analytics.aspx (Accessed March 18, 2016)

How do these various preceding concepts relate to business intelligence?

Figure 5-1

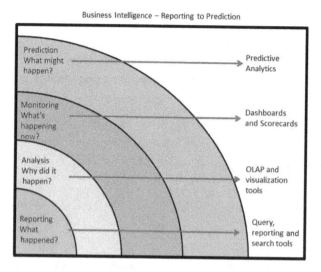

Note that the outside, white area beyond "Prediction" is the area where prescriptive analytics or "How can we make this happen?" occurs.

KNOWLEDGE CHECK

1. What is exploratory data analysis?

    a. Using statistical models for forecasting purposes.
    b. Affirming existing beliefs.
    c. Finding new characteristics in data.
    d. Prescribing actions to take.

WHAT PLATFORMS CAN BE USED FOR BIG DATA?

Figure 5-2: Big Data Architecture

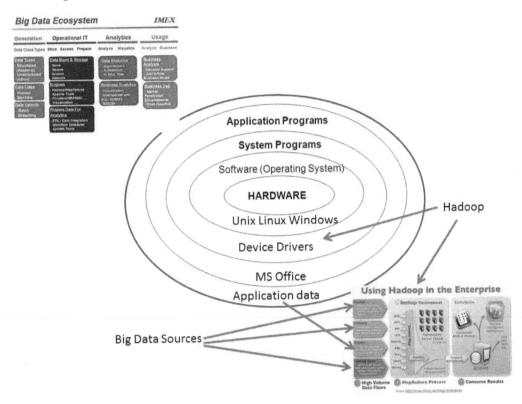

Let's begin with a review of the overall architecture of a Big Data system. This section will outline general concepts so that readers can relate their organization systems to the generic Big Data model.

Although figure 5-2 does not begin with strategy, it is at the forefront of all IT vision, objectives, hardware, and applications. It is foolish to acquire hardware or software or to discuss Big Data without addressing the strategic goals relating to information technology for the company. Therefore, the strategy is an essential component of a Big Data system.

Hardware and OS Selection

Hardware selection is at the core of a Big Data system. Most organizations will have established IT architecture. Big Data will address what is available, where the company would like to end up, and then create the plan to acquire the necessary hardware. One of the major tenants of Big Data is to use commodity computers (that regularly fail) that are connected to create distributed files and distributed applications. Based on your organization's Big Data approach, hardware will incorporate many commodity type computers. These will work with Hadoop (or selected system software)

Once you have selected hardware, you must select the operating system that will run on the hardware. The operating system is the main software that supports the computer's primary functions. Examples of operating systems are Windows, Linux, Unix, and iOS.

The next steps involve selecting the software programs that runs on the operating system. System programs have direct control of the computer and perform I/O memory operations. Examples of system programs are Device Drivers, BIOS software, HD Sector Boot Software, Assembler and compiler software. Hadoop, the program that enables Big Data, will be described in the following section.

Application programs are traditional accounting applications such as accounting packages, CRM, ERP, MS Office, iTunes, Adobe Photoshop, and the like. Big Data programs running in conjunction with Hadoop (also programs to reduce, curate, save, analyze, predict, report):

In the following section, we will explore application data that comes from several programs. Application data can be structured, semi-structured, or unstructured. Data from traditional programs are usually structured. Data from outside sources (government, industry, science) or from other media sources (pictures, images, video, audio) are usually semi-structured. Data from social media or from streaming sources such as machines, appliances, or sensors are usually unstructured. More confusingly, some software can function as more than one of the preceding applications. Figure 5-3 attempts to align software applications with the various segments of Big Data. This image is not meant to be all-encompassing but to show that the selection of software will be dependent on the applications an organization would like to perform.

Figure 5-3: Software Vendor Capabilities

Infrastructure	Data Organization & Management	Analytics and Discovery	Decision Support & Automation Interface
IBM			
Oracle			
	SAP		
HP			
Amazon			
Teradata			
EMC			
	SAS		
	Informatica		
	1010Data		
	Pervasive		
	Zettaset		
	MapR		
	Hstreaming		
	Hadoop		
	Cloudera		
	Karmaspher		
	HortonWorks		
	Datameer		

Businesses are confronted with growing quantities of data and increased expectations for analysis. In response, vendors are providing highly distributed architectures and new levels of memory and processing power. New entrants into the market are capitalizing on the open-source licensing model, which is becoming an essential component of Big Data software or architecture.

Apache Hadoop, an established open-source data processing platform was first used by Internet giants such as Yahoo and Facebook in 2006. Cloudera introduced commercial support for enterprises in 2008, and MapR and Hortonworks entered the market in 2009 and 2011, respectively. Among data-management veterans, IBM and EMC- Pivotal introduced their Hadoop distribution. Microsoft and Teradata offer complementary software and support for Hortonworks' platform. Oracle resells and supports Cloudera while HP, SAP, and others work with multiple Hadoop providers.

Real-time stream processing and stream-analysis are more achievable with Hadoop because of advances in bandwidth, memory, and processing power. However, this technology has yet to see broad adoption. Several vendors have complex event processing (complex event processing, or CEP for short, is not as complex at the name might suggest; fundamentally, CEP is about applying business rules to streaming event data),[1] but outside of the financial trading, national intelligence, and security communities, it has rarely been installed. There may be movement in applications in ad delivery, content personalization, logistics, and other areas as Big Data has broader adoption.[2]

KNOWLEDGE CHECK

2. Data from outside sources such as government or industry was listed as

   a. Structured.
   b. Unstructured.
   c. Semi-structured.
   d. Non-relational.

3. Which of the following was not listed as an infrastructure resource for Big Data?

   a. SAP.
   b. Oracle.
   c. IBM.
   d. HP.

Vendor Selection

Next, let's look at some well-known vendor choices for Big Data software along with brief comments about the software.

1. 1010data Facts is a hosted suite of data sets that allow access to disparate Big Data information sources. Also, it seamlessly integrates with company data. 1010data has access to a wide variety of external data, including consumer spending, e-commerce, weather, econometrics, transportation, and demographics. Data are granular, current, and can be manipulated very quickly.[3]

---

[1] https:/ / mapr.com/ blog/ better-complex-event-processing-scale-using-microservices-based-streaming-architecture-part-1/
[2] Wayne Eckerson, "Predictive Analytics," TDWI, May 10, 2007, https:/ / tdwi.org/ articles/ 2007/ 05/ 10/ predictive-analytics.aspx, Accessed 3/ 30/ 17
[3] "Datasets Overview," 1010 Data, https:/ / www.1010data.com/ products/ 1010facts/ 1010data-facts Accessed 3/ 30/ 17

2. Actian Vortex provides capabilities for realizing business value from Hadoop.[4] Its best in class data preparation and the broadest analytics support the following:
   - Elastic data preparation: Bring in all data quickly with the fastest analytic engines, data ingestion technology, and Konstanz Information Miner (KNIME) user interface
   - SQL analytics: Use SQL skills, applications, and tools with Hadoop for fully industrialized SQL support.
   - Predictive analytics: Uncover trends and patterns with hyper-parallelized Hadoop analytic operators powered by KNIME.

3. Amazon Web Services (AWS), began offering IT infrastructure services to businesses via cloud computing in 2006.[5] Cloud computing allows businesses to replace up-front infrastructure expenses (with no need to order servers and other infrastructure in weeks or months in advance) with lower and more variable costs that scale with the business within minutes.

   For example, AWS is a cloud service that is scalable and low-cost. There are hundreds of thousands of businesses in 190 countries around the world using AWS. They have data center locations in the United States, Europe, Brazil, Singapore, Japan, and Australia, and deliver the benefits such as low cost, agility, flexibility, and security to their customers:

4. Cloudera offers a unified platform for Big Data–the Enterprise Data Hub. Enterprises now have one place to store, process, and analyze all their data, empowering them to extend the value of existing investments while enabling fundamental new ways to derive value from their data.

   Founded in 2008, Cloudera was the first and is currently the leading provider and supporter of Apache Hadoop for the enterprise. Cloudera also offers software for business-critical data challenges including storage, access, management, analysis, security, and search.[6]

5. HP Big Data Services can help IT infrastructure to process increasing volumes of bytes—from emails, social media, and website downloads—and convert them into beneficial information. HP Big Data solutions encompass strategy, design, implementation, protection and compliance as follows:
   - Big Data Architecture Strategy: Define the functionalities and capabilities needed to align IT with Big Data initiatives. Through transformation workshops and roadmap services, learn to capture, consolidate, manage and protect business-aligned information, including structured, semi-structured and unstructured data.
   - Big Data System Infrastructure: HP will design and implement a high-performance, integrated platform to support a strategic architecture for Big Data. Services include design and implementation, reference architecture implementations and integration. A flexible, scalable infrastructure will support Big Data variety, consolidation, analysis, share and search on HP platforms.
   - Big Data Protection: Ensure availability, security, and compliance of Big Data systems. HP can help safeguard data, achieve regulatory compliance and lifecycle protection across the Big Data landscape, as well as improve backup and continuity measures.

6. Hortonworks Hadoop data platform (HDP) is the only completely open HDP available.[7] All solutions in HDP are developed as projects through the Apache Software Foundation (ASF). There

---

[4] "Hadoop is here to stay," Actian, www.actian.com/ products/ analytics-platform/ vortex-sql-hadoop-analytics/ Accessed 3/ 30/ 17

[5] "About AWS," Amazon Web Services, http:/ / aws.amazon.com/ about-aws, Accessed 3/ 30/ 17

[6] "FAQs About Cloudera," Cloudera, www.cloudera.com/ content/ cloudera/ en/ about/ faqs.html# one Accessed 3/ 30/ 17

[7] "Maximize the Value of Data at Rest," Hortonworks, hortonworks.com/ hdp/

are no proprietary extensions in HDP. HDP offers linear scale storage and computing across a wide range of access methods from batch to interactive, to real time, search, and streaming. It includes a comprehensive set of capabilities across governance, integration, security, and operations. HDP integrates with existing applications and systems to take advantage of Hadoop with only minimal changes to existing data architectures and skillsets. Deploy HDP in-cloud, on-premise, or from an appliance across both Linux and Windows.

7. IBM includes the following types of information management data and analytics capabilities:[8]
   * Data management and warehouse: Provide effective database performance across multiple workloads with lower administration, storage, development, and server costs; realize extreme speed with capabilities optimized for analytics workloads such as deep analytics; and benefit from workload-optimized systems that can be up and running in hours.
   * Hadoop system: Bring the power of Apache Hadoop to the enterprise with application accelerators, analytics, visualization, development tools, performance and security features.
   * Stream computing: Efficiently deliver real-time analytic processing on constantly changing data in motion and enable descriptive and predictive analytics to support real-time decisions. Capture and analyze all data, all the time, just in time; and, with stream computing, store less, analyze more, and make better decisions faster.
   * Content management: Enable comprehensive content lifecycle and document management with cost-effective control of existing and new types of content with scale, security, and stability.
   * Information integration and governance: Build confidence in big data with the ability to integrate, understand, manage, and govern data appropriately across its lifecycle.

8. Infobright is an analytic database platform for storing and analyzing machine-generated data.[9]
   * Data compression ratios of 20:1 to 40:1
   * Fast, consistent query performance even when data volumes increase dramatically.
   * Scale to hold terabytes and petabytes of historical data needed for long-term analytics.
   * Load speeds of terabytes per hour to provide for real-time query processing or alerting

9. Kognitio software which interoperates seamlessly with existing business integration and analytics reporting tools[10] and "data lakes" (large object-based storage repositories that hold data in native formats until needed)[11] and Hadoop storage. It complements the pre-existing technology stack, bridging the usability gap to the new large-volume data stores, helping achieve timely value from Big Data. The Kognitio Analytical Platform is a scale-out in-memory, massively parallel processing (MPP), not-only-SQL, software technology optimized for low-latency, large-volume data load, and high-throughput complex analytical workloads.

10. MapR is the only distribution system that is built from the ground up for business-critical production applications.[12]

MapR is a complete distribution for Apache Hadoop that includes more than a dozen projects from the Hadoop ecosystem to provide a broad set of Big Data capabilities. The MapR platform includes high availability, disaster recovery, security, and full data protection. In addition, MapR allows Hadoop to be easily accessed as traditional network attached storage with read-write capabilities.

---

[8] "Big Data at the Speed of Business," IBM, www-01.ibm.com/ software/ data/ bigdata/ , Accessed 3/ 30/ 17

[9] "Internet of Things," *InfoBright*, www.infobright.com/ index.php/ internet-of-things/ , Accessed 3/ 30/ 17

[10] "The Kognitio Analytic Platform," Kognitio, accessed March 18, 2016,kognitio.com/ analyticalplatform/ , Accessed 3/ 30/ 17

[11] "Data Lake," *TechTarget*, searchaws.techtarget.com/ definition/ data-lake, Accessed 3/ 30/ 17

[12] "What Is Apache Hadoop?" MapR, www.mapr.com/ products/ apache-hadoop, Accessed 3/ 30/ 17

11. Microsoft's vision is to enable all users to gain actionable insights from virtually any data, including insights previously hidden in unstructured data.[13] To achieve this, Microsoft is a comprehensive Big Data solution.

   - A modern data management layer that supports all data types—structured, semi-structured and unstructured data. It is easier to integrate, manage, and present real-time data streams, providing a more holistic view of the business and foster rapid decisions.
   - The software also has an enrichment layer that enhances data discovery, which combines the world's industry data with advanced analytics. The software can connect and import data, create visualizations, and run reports on a regular basis on the go.
   - The software has an insights layer using tools such as MS Office with rich 3D visualizations and storytelling built into its Excel program, which makes it easier to visualize multiple data sources and modify them on the fly while presenting in PowerPoint.
   - HD Insight is Microsoft's new Hadoop-based service built on the Hortonworks Data Platform that offers 100 percent compatibility with Apache Hadoop.

12. Oracle is a complete suite of infrastructure and software tools to address an organization's Big Data needs.

13. Pivotal Big Data Suite provides a broad foundation for agile data.[14] It can be deployed as part of the Pivotal Cloud Foundry or as PaaS (platform as a service) technologies, on-premise and in public clouds, in virtualized environments, on commodity hardware, or delivered as an appliance. The suite offers the following:

   - SQL analytics-optimized Hadoop based on ODP core
   - Leading analytical massively-parallel processing database
   - Massively-parallel processing, ANSI-compliant SQL on Hadoop query engine

14. Software such as SAP HANA can simplify IT architecture.[15] It combines in-memory processing with an enterprise data warehouse (EDW) and Hadoop to help harness Big Data. It purports to do the following:

   - Run business processes 10,000 to 100,000 times faster.
   - Use Big Data analytics with SAP IQ, a data warehouse solution.
   - Virtualize data across a logical Big Data warehouse and gain insight without moving data.

15. Teradata Aster has an analytic engine that is a native graph processing engine for Graph Analysis across Big Data sets.[16] Using this next generation analytic engine, organizations can solve complex business problems such as social network or influencer analysis, fraud detection, supply chain management, network analysis and threat detection, and money laundering.

16. A new generation of data analyst has made R the most popular analytic software in today's market. Teradata Aster R lifts the limitations of open-source R with pre-built parallel R functions, parallel constructors, and integration of open-source R in the Aster SNAP Framework.

   What is R? R is a language and environment for statistical computing and graphics. It is a GNU project which is similar to the S language and environment developed at Bell Laboratories (formerly AT&T, now Lucent Technologies). R can be considered as a different implementation of S. There are some important differences, but much code written for S runs unaltered under R.

   R provides a wide variety of statistical (linear and nonlinear modeling, classical statistical tests, time-series analysis, classification, clustering ...) and graphical techniques, and is highly

---

[13] Microsoft.com

[14] Pivotal.io

[15] SAP.com

[16] Teradata.com

extensible. The S language is often the vehicle of choice for research in statistical methodology, and R provides an open-source route to participation in that activity.

One of R's strengths is the ease with which well-designed publication-quality plots can be produced, including mathematical symbols and formulae where needed. Great care has been taken over the defaults for the minor design choices in graphics, but the user retains full control.

R is available as free software under the terms of the Free Software Foundation's GNU General Public License in source code form. It compiles and runs on a wide variety of UNIX platforms and similar systems (including FreeBSD and Linux), Windows and MacOS.[17]

Aster Discovery Platform also provides SQL and SQL-MapReduce analytic engines that enable a variety of analytics best suited to these engines, such as SQL analysis, path or pattern analysis, statistical analysis and text analysis.

KNOWLEDGE CHECK

4. What is MapR?

    a. A program to reduce the size of Big Data analyzed.
    b. Incomplete distribution of Apache Hadoop.
    c. Complete distribution for Apache Hadoop that packages more than a dozen projects.
    d. A relational database for Big Data.

5. What is Teradata?

    a. Agriculture applications of Big Data.
    b. Data analytics software.
    c. A native graph processing engine for graph analysis.
    d. A relational database.

TOP DATA ANALYSIS TOOLS FOR BUSINESS

The following list of top data analysis tools for business was based on guidelines set by Alex Jones of KDNuggets, a business analytics site. He suggests tools based on their "free availability (for personal use), ease of use (no coding and intuitively designed), powerful capabilities (beyond basic Excel), and well-documented resources," (such as simple Google searches to support business needs).[18]

1. Tableau, according to its website, is "business intelligence software that allows anyone to connect easily to data, and then visualize and create interactive, shareable dashboards. It's easy enough that any Excel user can learn it, but powerful enough to satisfy even the most complex analytical problems. Securely sharing your findings with others only takes seconds." The tool is simple and

---

[17] www.r-project.org
[18] "Top 10 Data Analysis Tools for Business," *KDNuggets*, www.kdnuggets.com/ 2014/ 06/ top-10-data-analysis-tools-business.html, Accessed 3/ 30/ 17

intuitive, and the public software version has a million-row limit that allows for extensive data analytics.[19]

2. OpenRefine (formerly Google Refine), according to its website, "cleans 'messy data and transforms it from one format into another; extending it with web services; and linking it to databases like Freebase." With the software, a user can do the following:
   - Import various data formats.
   - Explore datasets in a matter of seconds.
   - Apply basic and advanced cell transformations.
   - Deal with cells that contain multiple values.
   - Create instantaneous links between datasets.
   - Filter and partition data easily with regular expressions.
   - Use named-entity extraction on full-text fields to automatically identify topics.
   - Perform advanced data operations with the general refined expression language.[20]

3. KNIME can manipulate, analyze, and model data with visual programming. The user drags connection points between activities instead of writing blocks of code. The software can be extended to run R, Python, text mining, chemistry data, and the like, which provides the option to work in more advanced code-driven analysis.

4. RapidMiner operates through visual programming and can manipulate, analyze, and model data.

5. Google Fusion Tables is a versatile tool for data analysis, large data-set visualization, and mapping. Google has the leading mapping software. (See Google maps in the following sections of text.) Table 5-3 illustrates 2013 crime statistics from the FBI.[21] This image shows an example of the data that was available.

Table 5-3

| | | | | | | | | | | | | | |
| D109 | | | | fx | =Googlegeocode(C109) | | | | | | | | |

State	City	Population	Violent crime	Murder and nonnegligent manslaughter	Rape (revised definition)[1]	Rape (legacy definition)[2]	Robbery	Aggravated assault	Property crime	Burglary	Larceny-theft	Motor vehicle theft	Arson[3]
WISCONSIN	Adams	1,924	7	0	3		0	4	88	16	68	4	0
	Albany	1,015	8	0		0	0	8	46	11	34	1	0
	Algoma	3,143	1	0	1		0	0	83	1	81	1	0
	Alma	759	0	0		0	0	0	2	0	2	0	0
	Altoona	7,018	8	1		0	1	6	85	17	68	0	0
	Amery	2,859	11	0		0	0	11	36	6	27	3	0
	Antigo	7,988	10	0		0	0	10	419	77	329	13	0
	Appleton	73,141	176	1	28			14	133	1,304	186	1,088	30	15
	Arcadia	2,950	3	0		0	1	2	33	2	29	2	0
	Ashland	8,097	32	1		4	3	24	429	47	373	9	1
	Ashwaubenon	17,145	14	0		5	7	2	746	48	684	14	0
	Athens	1,100	0	0		0	0	0	7	1	6	0	0
	Avoca	636	0	0		0	0	0	18	2	16	0	0
	Bangor	1,494	3	0	1		0	2	11	0	11	0	0
	Baraboo	12,047	25	0		7	3	15	410	46	359	5	1
	Barneveld	1,238	0	0		0	0	0	18	3	13	2	0
	Bayfield	488	1	0		0	0	1	27	4	23	0	0
	Beaver Dam	16,326	8	0		0	1	7	575	104	470	1	2
	Belleville	2,436	1	0	0		0	1	30	2	28	0	0

Using Google Fusion Tables, the data was uploaded, and a map was created for the violent crime by city.

---

[19] Tableau.com

[20] OpenRefine.com

[21] "Crime in the U.S., 2013," Federal Bureau of Investigation website, www.fbi.gov/ about-us/ cjis/ ucr/ crime-in-the-u.s/ 2013/ crime-in-the-u.s.-2013

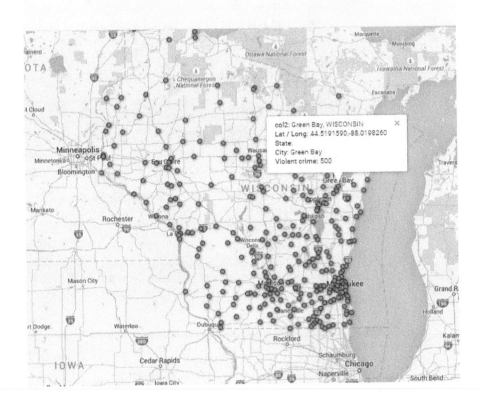

The author then clicked on the map to show the violent crime in the city of Green Bay for 2013.

6. NodeXL is a visualization and analysis software for networks and relationships. Chapter 6 illustrates an example of linked-in connections that is similar in concept. NodeXL takes that a step further by providing exact calculations. A simpler tool is also available. See the node graph on Google Fusion Tables, or (for a little more visualization) try out Gephi.

7. Import.io provides quick access to web data. The software highlights relevant data and (in a matter of minutes) "learns" what for the user is looking for. From there, Import.io will pull data for the user to analyze or export.

8. Google search operators are often an underused research tool. Operators allow the quick filtering of Google results to get to the most useful and relevant information. For instance, it is possible to obtain CFO survey information by accessing any of the major CPA firms' websites as follows:

Do not forget to leverage the power of the search by using additional tools such as the time search feature.

9. Solver is an optimization and linear programming tool in Excel that allows users to set constraints. It is not the strongest of optimization packages but will be most helpful if the company has never explored optimization analysis. For advanced optimization, consider a program such as R's optim package.

10. WolframAlpha's search engine is one of the web's hidden gems and helps to power Apple's Siri. WolframAlpha provides detailed responses to technical searches and makes quick work of calculus homework. WolframAlpha has been referred to as the "nerdy Google" for business users, as it presents information charts and graphs and is excellent for high-level pricing history, commodity information, and topic overviews.[22]

---

22 *KDNuggets*

11. Google Maps can be accessed at https://www.google.com/maps/d/, where the user selects "Create a new map"; then clicks "Import."

There will be an option to select a file from Google Drive or your computer. The author selected a recent CSV file that showed his speaking engagement cities over the last five years. Google Maps asked the author to identify which columns should be chosen for placemarks in the graph.

Choose columns to position your placemarks

Select the columns from your file that tell us where to put placemarks on the map, such as addresses or latitude-longitude pairs. All columns will be imported.

☐ date
☐ Client
☑ Course
☐ Title
☑ City
☑ State

Continue   Back   Cancel

Next, the application asked the user to identify a column to use as the title for the place-markers and "Course" was checked. The exported PDF looked like this:

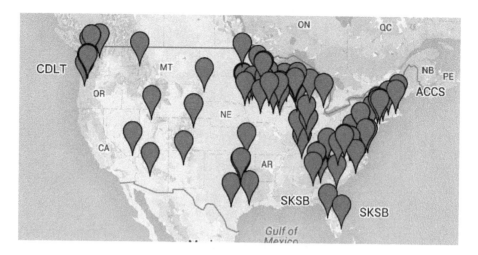

There was an option to customize the labels so that they could be highlighted differently by any of the columns listed previously. In the next image, the clients are labeled with different color place-markers.

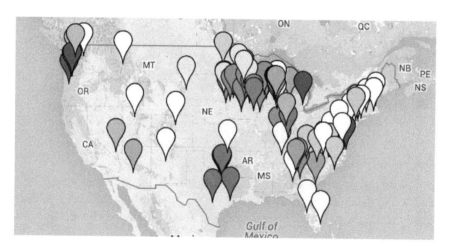

In the next image, the Midwest is enlarged.

In the next image, another option was activated. The option overlaid the place-markers with the course acronym taught. Some of the information is hard to read because of multiple dates and multiple courses delivered in a particular city.

The tool has many options including driving paths, adding place-markers, adding more layers, sharing with others, posting for public consumption, and the like.

KNOWLEDGE CHECK

6. What is Wolfram Alpha?

    a. Data analytics software.
    b. The nerdy Google.
    c. Predictive analytics software.
    d. A subprogram within the MapR framework.

7. Google Maps was illustrated using

    a. Consulting engagements.
    b. Crime statistics.
    c. Vendor dispersion.
    d. Post offices across the U.S.

HADOOP—WHAT IS IT ALL ABOUT?

The Apache Hadoop project develops open-source software for reliable, scalable, distributed computing. Hadoop is a framework with the ability to store large data sets. The data sets are distributed across clusters of computers using simple programming models and written in Java to run on a single computer or large clusters of commodity hardware computers. The software derives from papers published by Google and incorporates the features of the Google File System (GFS) and MapReduce paradigm, reflected in the names Hadoop Distributed File System and Hardtop MapReduce.

Hadoop technology was designed to eliminate the data handling problems on big data in companies and achieved great success. It can process huge amounts of data quickly from a variety of sites such as Facebook, Twitter, and the like, and automated sensors.

Hadoop Terminology

- Open-source software: Works on the open network of developers that create and manage the programs.
- Framework: Everything that enables users to develop and run software applications and is done through programs, tool sets, connections, and the like.
- Distributed data: Divided and stored on multiple computers, and computations can run simultaneously on multiple connected machines.
- Massive storage: The Hadoop framework can store enormous amounts of data in blocks for storage on clusters of low-cost commodity hardware.
- Faster processing: Processes large amounts of data in parallel across clusters of tightly connected low-cost computers for quick results.

KNOWLEDGE CHECK

8. Which of these describes Hadoop?

    a. It is proprietary.
    b. It is open source.
    c. It is proprietary but available for reduced costs to nonprofit organizations.
    d. It is proprietary and must run in a Unix environment.

History of Hadoop

Larger data demands have resulted in users wanting quicker searches and faster processing time. Doug Cutting and Mike Caferella worked on these issues with an open-source web search engine project called Nutch. They used distributed data and calculations across low-cost computers just to accomplish multiple tasks simultaneously. During the same period, Google was working on a similar project to achieve data storage and data processing in a distributed fashion to return faster and more relevant searches. In 2006, Cutting moved to Yahoo and continued with the Nutch project that was divided into two projects—the web crawler portion and the distributed processing portion (which became known as Hadoop).

Hadoop was released in 2008 as an open-source project that is managed and maintained by a non-profit Apache Software Foundation (ASF). The project is developed by a global community of software developers and contributors.

Apache Hadoop Ecosystem

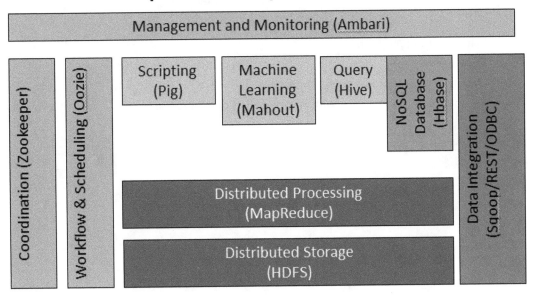

Source: "Big Data Basics "MSSQLTIPS, www.mssqltips.com/sqlservertip/3262/big-data-basics--part-6--related-apache-projects-in-hadoop-ecosystem/

These are the core components of Apache Software Foundation.

- HDFS: Java-based distributed file system that stores data such as structured, unstructured, and the like, without prior organization.
- MapReduce: Software model that allows large sets of data to be processed in parallel.
- YARN: Resource management framework to schedule and handle resource requests from distributed apps.
- Pig: Platform for manipulating data stored in HDFS. All this is done through a compiler called Pig Latin, for MapReduce programs and a high-level language. The user can avoid writing MapReduce programs to perform data extractions, transformations, loading, and basic analysis.
- Hive: Similar to database programming, it creates data in the form of tables. Hive is data warehousing and a query language.
- HBase: Runs on top of Hadoop and serves as input and output for MapReduce jobs. It is a non-relational distributed database.
- Zookeeper: Application meant for coordination of distributed processes.
- Ambari: Web interface meant for managing, configuring, and testing in the Hadoop environment.
- Flume: Software that collects, aggregates, and streams data into HDFS.
- Sqoop: Transfer mechanism for data moved between Hadoop and its relational database.
- Oozie: Hadoop job scheduler.

KNOWLEDGE CHECK

9. What is Hive?

    a. Data cleansing program.

    b. Data analytics tool.

    c. Data warehousing and a query language.

    d. An application meant for coordination of distributed processes.

Practice Questions

1. Based on the IBM survey, list several capabilities of Big Data.

2. What is the purpose of Hadoop?

3. What is the purpose of Map Reduce?

4. What is "R"?

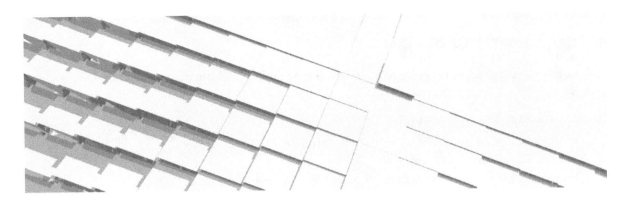

Chapter 6

BIG DATA END USER AND ACCOUNTING TOOLS

LEARNING OBJECTIVES

After completing this chapter, you should be able to do the following:

- Recognize how optimization is used with Big Data.
- Recall an actual example of Big Data in the electronics retail business.
- Identify other Big Data resources.

INTRODUCTION

This chapter examines accounting tools that can be used for Big Data analysis. The reader may be familiar with some of the tools but may not have considered the use of the tools as a resource for analyzing Big Data. One of these tools is very helpful in the analysis of generating sales and referrals. We'll start our discussion by examining the use of Big Data in a real-life example, using data pulled from a nationwide retailer. The example will illustrate how to access, dissect, and evaluate Big Data, both in terms of data contained in the information as well as inferences that can be drawn from the Big Data.

ACTUAL EXAMPLE OF BIG DATA

In this section, the participant is going to be involved in a real-life Big Data example. As you look at the example, keep in mind the following:

- Notice the "look" of real Big Data.
- Determine if any trends can be identified within the Big Data.
- Speculate on how the trends changed.
- Determine what management actions could be taken in view of the data.

EXAMPLE OF ACCESSING ACTUAL CORPORATE DATA—BEST BUY

Best Buy allows the public to access some of its Big Data. You can access the data by visiting https://developer.bestbuy.com/gallery.

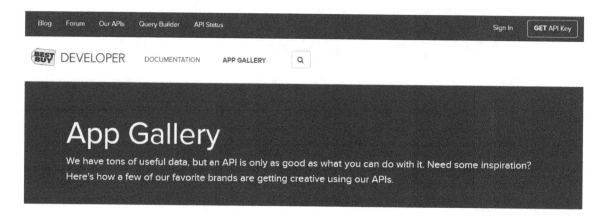

It is necessary to get an API key, so click on the upper right hand of the website where it says Get API Key. A key will be assigned to be used when accessing the applicable apps. Note the additional series of apps that can be used.

Query Builder

Query Builder helps users get the most out of the Best Buy APIs by creating custom queries. Create a base for your own custom queries or use the Query Builder to access Best Buy API data. You can even customize your responses to better serve your purpose.

IFTTT

IFTTT helps you create powerful connections with one simple statement: "If This, Then That". IFTTT has already integrated with Channels like Facebook, Evernote, LinkedIn, email and now Best Buy. With the Best Buy Channel, you can create IFTTT Recipes that include product price, trend and availability changes. Check out Best Buy's sample Recipes on IFTTT.

Factual

Factual's Global Places is a definitive database of listings for more than 65 million local businesses and points of interest in 50 countries. Global Places uses the Stores API to incorporate data on more than one thousand Best Buy store locations, giving access to dependable information for developers worldwide.

Listia

Listia is a popular online marketplace that allows users to post items they no longer need to earn credits that can be redeemed for items listed by other users or new merchandise posted by Best Buy and other retailers. By partnering with Listia, Best Buy is helping customers reduce clutter, rescuing still-usable electronics from landfills and finding good homes for new tech gear.

TrackIf

TrackIf is an innovative shopping aggregator that searches the web to find exactly the products you're looking for. TrackIf will scour its partner sites for the best bargain of the day as well as price-drop and supply notifications.

ShopSavvy

Best Buy's partnership with ShopSavvy allows customers to find low online prices even when shopping in store. Shoppers can scan in-store items using the ShopSavvy app to compare competitor prices, find sales, make online purchases and more.

CitiBank

Citibank's ThankYou® Rewards allow customers to earn points by using a participating credit card or checking account. Those points can be redeemed for a wide array of products, including tablets, gaming consoles and other electronics from Best Buy. Customers can pick up their purchases at the nearest Best Buy store or have the products shipped, making it a model of convenience for shoppers in all walks of life and a fantastic discovery tool for Best Buy customers.

jifiti

Jifiti is a clever app for anyone weary of dropping fruitless hints about that upcoming birthday or other event. A list of suggested gifts is presented to your event guests, and their gift lands as a virtual gift card in your email. It's a thoughtful gift that allows both giver and receiver flexibility in choosing their favorites.

Source: Best Buy website, https://developer.bestbuy.com/gallery

The following descriptions are from the preceding Best Buy image and define what each application does.

Query Builder

Query Builder helps users get the most out of the Best Buy APIs by creating custom queries. Create a base for your own custom queries or use the Query Builder to access Best Buy API data. You can even customize your responses to better serve your purpose.

IFTTT

IFTTT helps you create powerful connections with one simple statement: "If This, Then That." IFTTT has already integrated with channels like Facebook, Evernote, LinkedIn, email and now Best Buy. With the Best Buy channel, you can create IFTTT recipes that include product price, trend and availability changes. Check out Best Buy's sample recipes on IFTTT.

Factual

Factual's Global Places is a definitive database of listings for more than 65 million local businesses and points of interest in 50 countries. Global Places uses the store's API to incorporate data on more than one thousand Best Buy store locations, giving access to dependable information for developers worldwide.

Listia

Listia is a popular online marketplace that allows users to post items they no longer need to earn credits that can be redeemed for items listed by other users or new merchandise posted by Best Buy and other retailers. By partnering with Listia, Best Buy is helping customers reduce clutter, rescuing still-usable electronics from landfills and finding good homes for new tech gear.

TrackIf

TrackIf is an innovative shopping aggregator that searches the web to find exactly the products you're looking for. TrackIf will scour its partner sites for the best bargain of the day, as well as price-drop and supply notifications.

ShopSavvy

Best Buy's partnership with ShopSavvy allows customers to find low online prices even when shopping in store. Shoppers can scan in-store items using the ShopSavvy app to compare competitor prices, find sales, and make online purchases and more.

CitiBank

Citibank's ThankYou Rewards allow customers to earn points by using a participating credit card or checking account. Those points can be redeemed for a wide array of products, including tablets, gaming consoles and other electronics from Best Buy. Customers can pick up their purchases at the nearest Best Buy store or have the products shipped, making it a model of convenience for shoppers in all walks of life and a fantastic discovery tool for Best Buy customers.

Jifiti

Jifiti is a clever app for anyone weary of dropping fruitless hints about that upcoming birthday or other event. A list of suggested gifts is presented to your event guests and their gift lands as a virtual gift card in your email. It's a thoughtful gift that allows both giver and receiver flexibility in choosing their favorites.

CatalogSpree

The Best Buy Circular is just one of the hundreds of catalogs and flyers waiting for your perusal with the CatalogSpree app. Share catalogs with friends and sorts your favorites with ease.

CowBoom

The Best Buy CowBoom brand is a trusted source for new, pre-owned and refurbished consumer electronics. CowBoom uses the commerce API to place orders through Best Buy without having to leave the CowBoom site, providing consistent branding, timely order placement, and a smooth, simple user experience.

Best Buy App

The Best Buy App puts a Best Buy store in your pocket. Browse the entire catalog, read reviews, compare specs, track My Best Buy rewards points and more. You can even make purchases right from your phone for home delivery or in-store pickup.

RedLaser

The RedLaser app allows users to scan UPC and QR codes at most major retail stores and receive instant price comparison to direct you to the lowest available price, as well as any applicable coupons or special offers. You can even cut down on web browsing time by making your purchase within the application, and My Best Buy customers can even scan their cards for instant access to loyalty benefits.

FindTheBest

FindTheBest is an online research engine that provides detailed information on more than 2,000 topics, enabling people to research with confidence. FindTheBest leverages our Products API to include timely pricing and product details for Best Buy products.

After the author had received his key to access the data (via email), he returned to the gallery page referenced previously and clicked on Query Builder.

The following image depicts the process to access the Best Buy catalog.

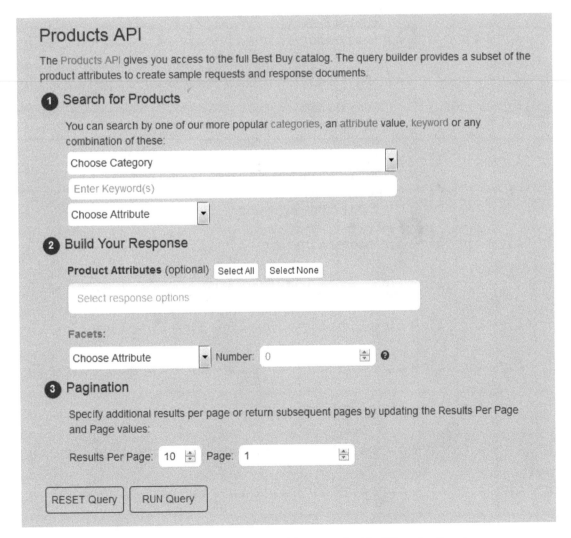

Source: Best Buy website, http://bestbuyapis.github.io/bby-query-builder/#/productSearch

---

Note that there are a number of options that can be included in the query, such as category and attribute. (See the following images.)

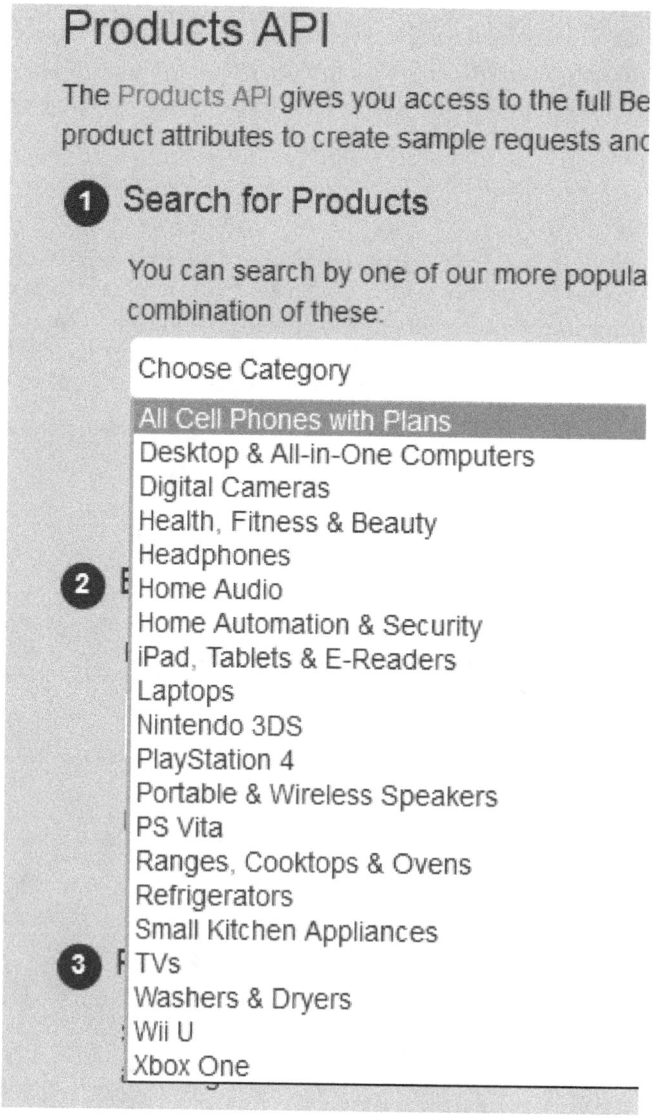

Products API

The Products API gives you access to the full Be
product attributes to create sample requests and

1 Search for Products

You can search by one of our more popula
combination of these:

Choose Category

All Cell Phones with Plans
Desktop & All-in-One Computers
Digital Cameras
Health, Fitness & Beauty
Headphones
Home Audio
Home Automation & Security
iPad, Tablets & E-Readers
Laptops
Nintendo 3DS
PlayStation 4
Portable & Wireless Speakers
PS Vita
Ranges, Cooktops & Ovens
Refrigerators
Small Kitchen Appliances
TVs
Washers & Dryers
Wii U
Xbox One

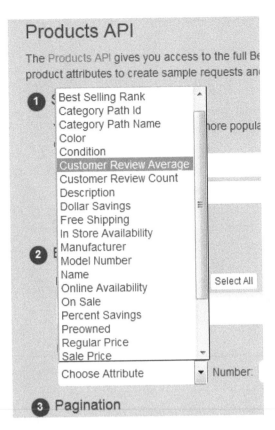

The author entered the data key and ran the query for the most viewed products. The following image shows the query detail.

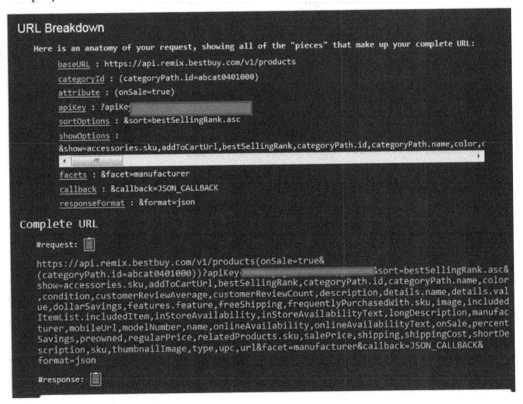

KNOWLEDGE CHECK

1. Query builder allows a user to do what?

    a. Perform "what if" analysis.
    b. Dispose of electronic items they no longer need
    c. To write custom queries for Best Buy products.
    d. Software to create, "If this, then that" statements for data analysis.

2. Which field was not available in the Best Buy attributes?

    a. Sales price.
    b. Regular price.
    c. Discount.
    d. Percent savings.

3. To allow the Best Buy query to run, what must a user do?

    a. Have access to data mining software.
    b. Obtain an API Key.
    c. Be able to read HTML.
    d. Obtain Best Buy field translator program.

EXERCISE

The following pages are meant to be included in the following format. It is difficult to read unless you have a background in IT, or you have a program that can automatically decipher the image. Therefore, the reader should spend several minutes alone or with a partner to digest the information. What do you notice in the details?

{ "metadata":{ "resultSet":{ "count":10} ,"context":{ "canonicalUrl":"http:/ / api.bestbuy.com/ beta/ product s/ mostViewed?apiKey= count"} } ,"results":[{ "customerReviews":{ "averageScore":"4.7","count":13308} ," descriptions":{ "short":"3rd generation; compatible with most HDTVs with an HDMI interface; allows you to stream movies, TV shows, photos and music from your computer to an HDTV or home theater system; 802.11a/ b/ g/ n wireless LAN. \ nLearn more about smart products."} ,"images":{ "standard":"http:/ / img.bbystatic.com/ BestBuy_US/ images/ products/ 4854/ 4854 433_sc.jpg"} ,"links":{ "product":"http:/ / api.remix.bestbuy.com/ v1/ products/ 4854433.json?apiKey= 56f gbf8desj1h7af8dfghjk6","web":"http:/ / www.bestbuy.com/ site/ apple-apple-tv-black/ 4854433.p?id= 1218552476525&skuId= 4854433&cmp= RMX&ky= 28eiIkWRnU6kpSRaThWcSId BYJmvGGbrI","addToCart":"http:/ / www.bestbuy.com/ site/ olspage.jsp?id= pcmcat152200050035&type = category&cmp= RMX&ky= 28eiIkWRnU6kpSRaThWcSIdBYJmvGGbrI&qvsids= 4854433"} ,"names": { "title":"Apple® - Apple TV® - Black"} ,"prices":{ "current":69.99,"regular":69.99} ,"rank":2,"sku":"4854433"} ,{ "customerReviews":{ "ave rageScore":"4.4","count":475} ,"descriptions":{ "short":"Tracks steps taken, distance traveled, calories burned, stairs climbed, elapsed time and sleep metrics; wrist-based heart rate monitoring; call notifications; backlit display"} ,"images":{ "standard":"http:/ / img.bbystatic.com/ BestBuy_US/ images/ products/ 8681/ 868153 3_sc.jpg"} ,"links":{ "product":"http:/ / api.remix.bestbuy.com/ v1/ products/ 8681533.json?apiKey= 56fgbf 8desj1h7af8dfghjk6","web":"http:/ / www.bestbuy.com/ site/ fitbit-charge-hr-heart-rate-and-activity-

tracker-sleep-wristband-small-
black/ 8681533.p?id= 1219357512977&skuId= 8681533&cmp= RMX&ky= 28eiIkWRnU6kpSRaThWcSId
BYJmvGGbrI","addToCart":"http:/ / www.bestbuy.com/ site/ olspage.jsp?id= pcmcat152200050035&type
= category&cmp= RMX&ky= 28eiIkWRnU6kpSRaThWcSIdBYJmvGGbrI&qvsids= 8681533"} ,"names":
{ "title":"Fitbit - Charge HR Heart Rate and Activity Tracker + Sleep Wristband (Small) -
Black"} ,"prices":{ "current":149.99,"regular":149.99} ,"rank":7,"sku":"8681533"} ,{ "customerReviews":{ "a
verageScore":"4.1","count":75} ,"descriptions":{ "short":"Windows 8.1Technical details: AMD A8-Series
processor; 15.6\ " display; 6GB memory; 500GB hard driveSpecial features: Bluetooth; HDMI
output"} ,"images":{ "standard":"http:/ / img.bbystatic.com/ BestBuy_US/ images/ products/ 2996/ 299602
6_sc.jpg"} ,"links":{ "product":"http:/ / api.remix.bestbuy.com/ v1/ products/ 2996026.json?apiKey= 56fgbf
8desj1h7af8dfghjk6","web":"http:/ / www.bestbuy.com/ site/ lenovo-15-6-laptop-amd-a8-series-6gb-
memory-500gb-hard-drive-
black/ 2996026.p?id= 1219567191659&skuId= 2996026&cmp= RMX&ky= 28eiIkWRnU6kpSRaThWcSId
BYJmvGGbrI","addToCart":"http:/ / www.bestbuy.com/ site/ olspage.jsp?id= pcmcat152200050035&type
= category&cmp= RMX&ky= 28eiIkWRnU6kpSRaThWcSIdBYJmvGGbrI&qvsids= 2996026"} ,"names":
{ "title":"Lenovo - 15.6\ " Laptop - AMD A8-Series - 6GB Memory - 500GB Hard Drive -
Black"} ,"prices":{ "current":329.99,"regular":329.99} ,"rank":10,"sku":"2996026"} ,{ "customerReviews":{ "
averageScore":null,"count":null} ,"descriptions":{ "short":"10.8\ " LCD touch screen with 1920 x 1280
resolutionWindows 8.1 operating system128GB storage capacityQuad-core processorWi-FiBluetooth
interface"} ,"images":{ "standard":"http:/ / img.bbystatic.com/ BestBuy_US/ images/ products/ 4968/ 49680
16_sc.jpg"} ,"links":{ "product":"http:/ / api.remix.bestbuy.com/ v1/ products/ 4968016.json?apiKey= 56fg
bf8desj1h7af8dfghjk6","web":"http:/ / www.bestbuy.com/ site/ microsoft-surface-3-10-8-intel-atom-
128gb-
silver/ 4968016.p?id= 1219645631904&skuId= 4968016&cmp= RMX&ky= 28eiIkWRnU6kpSRaThWcSId
BYJmvGGbrI","addToCart":"http:/ / www.bestbuy.com/ site/ olspage.jsp?id= pcmcat152200050035&type
= category&cmp= RMX&ky= 28eiIkWRnU6kpSRaThWcSIdBYJmvGGbrI&qvsids= 4968016"} ,"names":
{ "title":"Microsoft - Surface 3 - 10.8\ " - Intel Atom - 128GB -
Silver"} ,"prices":{ "current":599.99,"regular":599.99} ,"rank":3,"sku":"4968016"} ,{ "customerReviews":{ "a
verageScore":null,"count":null} ,"descriptions":{ "short":"10.8\ " LCD touch screen with 1920 x 1280
resolutionWindows 8.1 operating system64GB storage capacityQuad-core processorWi-FiBluetooth
interface"} ,"images":{ "standard":"http:/ / img.bbystatic.com/ BestBuy_US/ images/ products/ 4967/ 49670
17_sc.jpg"} ,"links":{ "product":"http:/ / api.remix.bestbuy.com/ v1/ products/ 4967017.json?apiKey= 56fg
bf8desj1h7af8dfghjk6","web":"http:/ / www.bestbuy.com/ site/ microsoft-surface-3-10-8-intel-atom-64gb-
silver/ 4967017.p?id= 1219645630549&skuId= 4967017&cmp= RMX&ky= 28eiIkWRnU6kpSRaThWcSId
BYJmvGGbrI","addToCart":"http:/ / www.bestbuy.com/ site/ olspage.jsp?id= pcmcat152200050035&type
= category&cmp= RMX&ky= 28eiIkWRnU6kpSRaThWcSIdBYJmvGGbrI&qvsids= 4967017"} ,"names":
{ "title":"Microsoft - Surface 3 - 10.8\ " - Intel Atom - 64GB -
Silver"} ,"prices":{ "current":499.99,"regular":499.99} ,"rank":1,"sku":"4967017"} ,{ "customerReviews":{ "a
verageScore":"4.6","count":2081} ,"descriptions":{ "short":"12\ " touch screen with 2160 x 1440
resolutionWindows 8.1 Pro operating system128GB storage capacity4th generation Intel&# 174;
Core&# 8482; i5 ProcessorMulti-position
Kickstand"} ,"images":{ "standard":"http:/ / img.bbystatic.com/ BestBuy_US/ images/ products/ 6243/ 624
3045_sc.jpg"} ,"links":{ "product":"http:/ / api.remix.bestbuy.com/ v1/ products/ 6243045.json?apiKey= 56
fgbf8desj1h7af8dfghjk6","web":"http:/ / www.bestbuy.com/ site/ microsoft-surface-pro-3-12-intel-core-i5-
128gb-
silver/ 6243045.p?id= 1219198824874&skuId= 6243045&cmp= RMX&ky= 28eiIkWRnU6kpSRaThWcSId
BYJmvGGbrI","addToCart":"http:/ / www.bestbuy.com/ site/ olspage.jsp?id= pcmcat152200050035&type
= category&cmp= RMX&ky= 28eiIkWRnU6kpSRaThWcSIdBYJmvGGbrI&qvsids= 6243045"} ,"names":
{ "title":"Microsoft - Surface Pro 3 - 12\ " - Intel Core i5 - 128GB -

---

Silver"},"prices":{"current":999.99,"regular":999.99},"rank":8,"sku":"6243045"},{"customerReviews":{"averageScore":"4.0","count":805},"descriptions":{"short":"Compatible with off-air HDTV broadcasts; retractable VHF dipoles; UHF loop"},"images":{"standard":"http://img.bbystatic.com/BestBuy_US/images/products/8280/8280834_sc.jpg"},"links":{"product":"http://api.remix.bestbuy.com/v1/products/8280834.json?apiKey=56fgbf8desj1h7af8dfghjk6","web":"http://www.bestbuy.com/site/rca-indoor-off-air-hdtv-antenna/8280834.p?id=1171058630499&skuId=8280834&cmp=RMX&ky=28eiIkWRnU6kpSRaThWcSIdBYJmvGGbrI","addToCart":"http://www.bestbuy.com/site/olspage.jsp?id=pcmcat152200050035&type=category&cmp=RMX&ky=28eiIkWRnU6kpSRaThWcSIdBYJmvGGbrI&qvsids=8280834"},"names":{"title":"RCA - Indoor Off-Air HDTV Antenna"},"prices":{"current":3.99,"regular":9.99},"rank":4,"sku":"8280834"},{"customerReviews":{"averageScore":"4.6","count":1466},"descriptions":{"short":"1080p resolutionClear Motion Rate 120Smart TVENERGY STAR Certified"},"images":{"standard":"http://img.bbystatic.com/BestBuy_US/images/products/5674/5674002_sc.jpg"},"links":{"product":"http://api.remix.bestbuy.com/v1/products/5674002.json?apiKey=56fgbf8desj1h7af8dfghjk6","web":"http://www.bestbuy.com/site/samsung-40-class-40-diag--led-1080p-smart-hdtv-black/5674002.p?id=1219146763131&skuId=5674002&cmp=RMX&ky=28eiIkWRnU6kpSRaThWcSIdBYJmvGGbrI","addToCart":"http://www.bestbuy.com/site/olspage.jsp?id=pcmcat152200050035&type=category&cmp=RMX&ky=28eiIkWRnU6kpSRaThWcSIdBYJmvGGbrI&qvsids=5674002"},"names":{"title":"Samsung - 40\" Class (40\" Diag.) - LED - 1080p - Smart - HDTV - Black"},"prices":{"current":379.99,"regular":479.99},"rank":6,"sku":"5674002"},{"customerReviews":{"averageScore":"4.6","count":733},"descriptions":{"short":"1080p resolutionClear Motion Rate 240Smart TV, Samsung Smart Hub, Web browser includedENERGY STAR Certified"},"images":{"standard":"http://img.bbystatic.com/BestBuy_US/images/products/6594/6594118_sc.jpg"},"links":{"product":"http://api.remix.bestbuy.com/v1/products/6594118.json?apiKey=56fgbf8desj1h7af8dfghjk6","web":"http://www.bestbuy.com/site/samsung-60-class-60-diag--led-1080p-smart-hdtv-black/6594118.p?id=1219226753264&skuId=6594118&cmp=RMX&ky=28eiIkWRnU6kpSRaThWcSIdBYJmvGGbrI","addToCart":"http://www.bestbuy.com/site/olspage.jsp?id=pcmcat152200050035&type=category&cmp=RMX&ky=28eiIkWRnU6kpSRaThWcSIdBYJmvGGbrI&qvsids=6594118"},"names":{"title":"Samsung - 60\" Class (60\" Diag.) - LED - 1080p - Smart - HDTV - Black"},"prices":{"current":849.99,"regular":1199.99},"rank":9,"sku":"6594118"},{"customerReviews":{"averageScore":null,"count":null},"descriptions":{"short":"DLP480p3D not enabled100 lumens white brightness, 100 lumens color brightnessSpeakers included"},"images":{"standard":"http://img.bbystatic.com/BestBuy_US/images/products/5036/5036011_sc.jpg"},"links":{"product":"http://api.remix.bestbuy.com/v1/products/5036011.json?apiKey=56fgbf8desj1h7af8dfghjk6","web":"http://www.bestbuy.com/site/zte-spro-dlp-wireless-smart-projector-black/5036011.p?id=1219645630545&skuId=5036011&cmp=RMX&ky=28eiIkWRnU6kpSRaThWcSIdBYJmvGGbrI","addToCart":"http://www.bestbuy.com/site/olspage.jsp?id=pcmcat152200050035&type=category&cmp=RMX&ky=28eiIkWRnU6kpSRaThWcSIdBYJmvGGbrI&qvsids=5036011"},"names":{"title":"ZTE - SPro DLP Wireless Smart Projector - Black"},"prices":{"current":399.99,"regular":449.99},"rank":5,"sku":"5036011"}]}

This exercise was included to display the type of information that is being gathered in structured terms that we do not typically access. Here is where it gets interesting. The preceding data are from May 5, 2015. The data were captured and brought into Excel. The data were parsed and the desired information was extracted to make it more user-friendly. Then, the same report was run two days later (May 7) and put into the same Excel worksheet. The following images represent one large image—the far most left and far most right of the data.)

A14 | fx | customerReviews":{"averageScore":"4.7","count":13332}, "descriptions":[{"short":"3rd generation; compatible with most HDTVs with an HDMI interface; allows you to stream movies, TV shows, photos and music

| A | B | C | D | E | F | G | H | I | J | K | L | M | N | O | P | Q | R |

1 5-May

2 customerReviews":{"averageScore":"4.7","count":13308}, "descriptions":[{"short":"3rd generation; compatible with most HDTVs with an HDMI interface; allows you to stream movies, TV shows, phot

3 customerReviews":{"averageScore":"4.4","count":475}, "descriptions":[{"short":"Tracks steps taken, distance traveled, calories burned, stairs climbed, elapsed time and sleep metrics; wrist-based hear

4 customerReviews":{"averageScore":"4.1","count":75}, "descriptions":[{"short":"Windows 8.1Technical details: AMD A8-Series processor; 15.6\" display; 6GB memory; 500GB hard driveSpecial feature

5 customerReviews":{"averageScore":null, "count":null}, "descriptions":[{"short":"10.8\" LCD touch screen with 1920 x 1280 resolutionWindows 8.1 operating system128GB storage capacityQuad-core p

6 customerReviews":{"averageScore":null, "count":null}, "descriptions":[{"short":"10.8\" LCD touch screen with 1920 x 1280 resolutionWindows 8.1 operating system64GB storage capacityQuad-core generat

7 customerReviews":{"averageScore":"4.6","count":2081}, "descriptions":[{"short":"12\" touch screen with 2160 x 1440 resolutionWindows 8.1 Pro operating system128GB storage capacity4th generat

8 customerReviews":{"averageScore":"4.0","count":805}, "descriptions":[{"short":"Compatible with off-air HDTV broadcasts; retractable VHF dipoles; UHF loop"}, "images":[{"standard":"http://img.bbyst

9 customerReviews":{"averageScore":"4.6","count":1466}, "descriptions":[{"short":"1080p resolutionClear Motion Rate 120Smart TVENERGY STAR Certified"}, "images":[{"standard":"http://img.bbystatic

10 customerReviews":{"averageScore":"4.6","count":733}, "descriptions":[{"short":"1080p resolutionClear Motion Rate 240Smart TV, Samsung Smart Hub, Web browser includedENERGY STAR Certified"}, "images":[{"stanc

11 customerReviews":{"averageScore":null, "count":null}, "descriptions":[{"short":"DLP480p3D not enabled100 lumens white brightness, 100 lumens color brightnessSpeakers included"}, "images":[{"stanc

12

13 7-May

14 customerReviews":{"averageScore":"4.7","count":13332}, "descriptions":[{"short":"3rd generation; compatible with most HDTVs with an HDMI interface; allows you to stream movies, TV shows, phot

15 customerReviews":{"averageScore":"4.9","count":826}, "descriptions":[{"short":"All-occasion gift card; shipped free; no expiration date or fees; safeguards against theft protect your purchase; good to

16 customerReviews":{"averageScore":"4.1","count":81}, "descriptions":[{"short":"Windows 8.1Technical details: AMD A8-Series processor; 15.6\" display; 6GB memory; 500GB hard driveSpecial feature

17 customerReviews":{"averageScore":"4.5","count":195}, "descriptions":[{"short":"Qualcomm Snapdragon 800 2.26GHz quad-core processorAndroid 4.2.2 Jelly Bean operating system4G LTE speedWi-F

18 customerReviews":{"averageScore":"4.7","count":3}, "descriptions":[{"short":"10.8\" LCD touch screen with 1920 x 1280 resolutionWindows 8.1 operating system128GB storage capacityQuad-core pr

19 customerReviews":{"averageScore":null, "count":null}, "descriptions":[{"short":"10.8\" LCD touch screen with 1920 x 1280 resolutionWindows 8.1 operating system64GB storage capacityQuad-core pr

20 customerReviews":{"averageScore":"4.0","count":805}, "descriptions":[{"short":"Compatible with off-air HDTV broadcasts; retractable VHF dipoles; UHF loop"}, "images":[{"standard":"http://img.bbystatic

21 customerReviews":{"averageScore":"4.6","count":1467}, "descriptions":[{"short":"1080p resolutionClear Motion Rate 120Smart TVENERGY STAR Certified"}, "images":[{"standard":"http://img.bbystatic

22 customerReviews":{"averageScore":"4.6","count":733}, "descriptions":[{"short":"1080p resolutionClear Motion Rate 240Smart TV, Samsung Smart Hub, Web browser includedENERGY STAR Certified"}, "images":[{"stanc

23 customerReviews":{"averageScore":"4.1","count":52}, "descriptions":[{"short":"Lets you dewrinkle, refresh, restore and preserve clothes in as little as 10 minutes; safe for use with most fabric types; ir

24

#	Content
1	y
2	FWRnU6kpSRaThWcSldBYImvGGbrl&qvsids=4854433"], "names":[{"title":"Apple® - Apple TV® - Black"}, "prices":[{"current":69.99, "regular":69.99}, "rank":2, "sku":"4854433"}, {"
3	Fbrl&qvsids=8681533"]}, "names":[{"title":"Fitbit - Charge HR Heart Rate and Activity Tracker + Sleep Wristband (Small) - Black"}, "prices":[{"current":149.99, "regular":149.99}, "rank":7, "sku":"8681533"}, {"
4	Fames":[{"title":"Lenovo - 15.6\" Laptop - AMD A8-Series - 6GB Memory - 500GB Hard Drive - Black"}, "prices":[{"current":329.99, "regular":329.99}, "rank":10, "sku":"2996026"}, {"
5	Microsoft - Surface 3 - 10.8\" - Intel Atom - 128GB - Silver"}, "prices":[{"current":599.99, "regular":599.99}, "rank":3, "sku":"4968016"}, {"
6	Frosoft - Surface 3 - 10.8\" - Intel Atom - 64GB - Silver"}, "prices":[{"current":499.99, "regular":499.99}, "rank":1, "sku":"4967017"}, {"
7	Fqvsids=6243045"]}, "names":[{"title":"Microsoft - Surface Pro 3 - 12\" - Intel Core i5 - 128GB - Silver"], "prices":[{"current":999.99, "regular":999.99}, "rank":8, "sku":"6243045"}, {"
8	F"8280834"}, {"
9	Fprices":[{"current":379.99, "regular":479.99}, "rank":6, "sku":"5674002"}, {"
10	flag.) - LED - 1080p - Smart - HDTV - Black"}, "prices":[{"current":849.99, "regular":1199.99}, "rank":9, "sku":"6594118"}, {"
11	F"current":399.99, "regular":449.99}, "rank":5, "sku":"5036011"}]}
12	
13	y
14	WRnU6kpSRaThWcSldBYImvGGbrl&qvsids=4854433"], "names":[{"title":"Apple® - Apple TV® - Black"], "prices":[{"current":69.99, "regular":69.99}, "rank":2, "sku":"4854433"}, {"
15	F["title":"Best Buy GC - $15 Gift Card"], "prices":[{"current":15.0, "regular":15.0}, "rank":9, "sku":"6263962"}, {"
16	Fames":[{"title":"Lenovo - 15.6\" Laptop - AMD A8-Series - 6GB Memory - 500GB Hard Drive - Black"], "prices":[{"current":329.99, "regular":329.99}, "rank":10, "sku":"2996026"}, {"
17	Frizon Wireless)"], "prices":[{"current":149.99, "regular":199.99}, "rank":4, "sku":"1723195"}, {"
18	Microsoft - Surface 3 - 10.8\" - Intel Atom - 128GB - Silver"], "prices":[{"current":599.99, "regular":599.99}, "rank":5, "sku":"4968016"}, {"
19	Frosoft - Surface 3 - 10.8\" - Intel Atom - 64GB - Silver"], "prices":[{"current":499.99, "regular":499.99}, "rank":3, "sku":"4967017"}, {"
20	C F"8280834"}, {"
21	Frprices":[{"current":379.99, "regular":479.99}, "rank":7, "sku":"5674002"}, {"
22	flag.) - LED - 1080p - Smart - HDTV - Black"], "prices":[{"current":849.99, "regular":1199.99}, "rank":8, "sku":"6594118"}, {"
23	F=7778016"], "names":[{"title":"SWASH - Express Clothing Care System - Linen"], "prices":[{"current":499.99, "regular":499.99}, "rank":1, "sku":"7778016"}]}
24	

Contrast May 5 with May 7. What can you find that is particularly interesting?

_____

_____

_____

_____

_____

_____

_____

_____

_____

_____

What have we learned from this search?

- The top 10 products.
- How the products are ranked.
- What the current price is.
- The original sales price.
- This report can be evaluated over different sales periods.

What uses can we make of this data?

- It can be compared to what consumers are searching for in other stores.
- It can be evaluated at different times (pre- and post-holiday.)
- It can be used to identify immediate price changes.
- It can also be used to show immediate product interest changes with the consumer.
- It can be related to actual sales in the future (predictive).
- It can be related to flyers sent out.
- It can be related to product positioning on the website.
- It can be related to special offers on the website.
- It is especially interesting to note the uptick in gift cards and the laundry appliance. There was no indication on May 5 that either the gift cards or laundry appliance were a top-viewed product. However, on May 7 both of these items moved into the top categories. Is it possible that this information reflects potential gifts for Mother's Day? (Note: When obtaining the permission to include the Best Buy data, the author discussed this insight with the Best Buy representative. The author was leading up to this point when the Best Buy representative said "Mother's Day.")

There are many other conclusions and inferences that can be made from the data; however, it should be apparent that insights are possible from data that was previously untracked. It would be intriguing to see the actual sales results over the next couple of weeks and see if there is a correlation between the top products viewed to the actual sales made. Also, consider this information from the perspective of a competitor. The competitor does not even need to send in a "mystery shopper." The data are available for comparative purposes.

OPTIMIZATION

One-size pricing rarely, if ever, fits all customers. There are many different determinants of pricing, which include the following:

- Commodity versus non-commodity status
- Availability of product
- Substitute products available
- Volumes purchased
- Seasonality
- Related products purchased
- Special discounts
- Customization required
- Lead time
- Expiration of product
- Quality of product
- Brand perception
- Competitor's pricing tactics
- Government laws
- Raw material price changes
- Other cost changes that must be passed on through pricing of product
- Version of product
- Where and how the product is sold (discount retailer versus high-end boutique)

Regardless of the characteristics, the seller must be aware of how these items interact and what the effect of product pricing is. If the product pricing is too high, margins may be obtained; but overall volume may decrease to the point that total revenue and profitability suffers. If the product pricing is too low, margins may suffer; but overall volume may increase to the point that total revenue and profitability may improve. Each of the characteristics can also affect the other features. For example, a customer that desires a prestigious product will expect a high price to limit the number of customers. If everyone can purchase the product, some customers will not see it as prestigious and, therefore, will not buy. The art in price setting, therefore, is to select the pricing methodology that complements the desired strategy to sell the product.

CRUISE LINE USES BIG DATA TO OPTIMIZE PRICES[1]

If characteristics are understood, how can Big Data complement the price setting process to optimize an organization's revenue? Let us examine how Carnival Cruise Lines made this happen.

---

[1] Kim Nash, "Carnival Strategy Chief Bets That Big Data Will Optimize Prices," The CIO Report, *The Wall Street Journal,* accessed March 21, 2016, http://blogs.wsj.com/cio/2015/04/30/carnival-strategy-chief-bets-that-big-data-will-optimize-prices/

Carnival Cruises wanted to segment its customer base to understand its spending patterns better. Carnival's goals were to learn the following:

- How to attract new customers
- How to re-price tickets to fill more staterooms
- Understanding customer's spending habits on souvenirs, excursions, and extras.

To glean this information, Carnival implemented a pioneering process. The company decided to employ data scientists to analyze data, economic trends, and social trends from past customers and vacationers in general. One objective was to match clients with the most appropriate cruise ship in its fleet of 100 ships—nine brands from budget family to luxury cruises. Differentiation of customers in terms of services and related price ranges could be significant.

Because the overall profitability of the cruise is dependent on the entire cruise, the company must be able to monitor and adjust strategies that can have a daily impact. Prices may not change dynamically, but the daily results may alter strategies and promotions.

The primary metric in the cruise business is available passenger cruise days (the number of days customers are aboard ship.) According to the CEO, the total available days over the fleet is 80 million in a year. In simple terms, if every passenger spent $1 more per day during his or her trip, Carnival would add $80 million in revenue over the course of one year.

The data science team at Carnival works daily, analyzing data such as passenger behavior, vacation trends, and questions from travel agents and queries from customers. The analysis runs overnight and develops thousands of recommendations for changes to ticket prices around the world. As an example, based on projected demand, the company can change the number of reservations allocated for different ports. In addition, this analysis may also result in shifting ship capacity from one country to another country across the ocean.

Carnival understands that analytics does not mean that they are making the correct decision—only a better-informed decision. Management still relies on their human experience in addition to analytics.

Is Carnival's approach working? The company's performance would suggest it is. Carnival reported record earnings in the third quarter of 2015 and is planning to add more ships to its fleet in 2016.

KNOWLEDGE CHECK

4. Carnival Cruises stresses that use of analytics to affect pricing will do what?

    a. Ensure that the best decision is made.
    b. Result in the highest possible price to be charged.
    c. Guarantee a better-informed decision.
    d. Guarantee that all options will be evaluated.

PREDICTIVE TOOLS

There are many tools that can be used to predict future outcomes. For example, what would be the advantage if we could predict the following?

1. The probability that a customer will refer other prospects.
2. The probability that a client will buy other products.
3. The likelihood of an employee to refer other prospective employees.
4. The likelihood of an employee to leave.

Basically, each of these questions would be possible to assess with data that we already have or could easily obtain. For instance, we could assess the likelihood in items 1. and 2. through customer surveys. We could assess items 3. and 4. by employee surveys or possibly even by employee email.

First, consider a tool that can be a predictor of corporate growth. The data that are used to predict this information may already be in the company system, or the data may exist in written (survey form) or may be determined by another type of feedback such as a customer follow-up call. This tool is known as the *Net Promoter Score* (NSP).

Frederick Reichheld of Bain Consulting developed the NSP in 2003. The simplicity of the NSP approach, as opposed to traditional customer surveys, originated with Enterprise Rental Car customer survey of two questions. Reichheld's research shows that there is a strong correlation between a company's growth rate and the percentage of customers who are "promoters."

KNOWLEDGE CHECK

5. Who created the Net Promoter Score?

    a. Lencione.
    b. Reichheld.
    c. Collins.
    d. Champy.

ENTERPRISE PREDICTIVE ANALYTIC TOOLS—2014[2]

There are a variety of software tools to generate predictive analytics. This section is not intended as a recommendation but only offers examples of some big names and basic comments.

Revolution Analytics: www.revolutionanalytics.com/

IBM Predictive Analytics: www-01.ibm.com/ software/ analytics/ spss/

---

[2] Enterprise Predictive Analytics Comparison 2014, Butler Analytics, accessed March 22, 2016, www.butleranalytics.com/ enterprise-predictive-analytics-comparisons-2014/

Actian: www.actian.com

FICO: www.fico.com/ en/ solutions/ big-data-analytics-decision-application-development-management/

SAS: www.sas.com/ en_us/ software/ analytics.html

Angoss: www.angoss.com

KNIME: https:/ / www.knime.org/

RapidMiner: http:/ / rapidminder.com

Alpine Data Labs: http:/ / alpinenow.com/

Salford Systems: https:/ / www.salford-systems.com/

SAP InfiniteInsight: http:/ / go.sap.com/ product/ analytics/ predictive-analytics.html

Blue Yonder: www.blue-yonder.com/ en/

Dotplot: www.dotplot.com

Oracle: www.oracle.com/ us/ products/ database/ options/ advanced-analytics/ overview/ index.html

BigML: http:/ / bigml.com

STATISTICA: www.statsoft.com/

OTHER SIMPLE TOOLS TO ACCESS BIG DATA SOURCES

Attendees of the AICPA's Controllers Annual Update received G17, which is an excellent source of data that supports the Industrial Production Statistics. It is issued monthly by the Federal Reserve. The following image represents the actual monthly production statistics by year for the overall index. The web reference is www.federalreserve.gov/ RELEASES/ g17/ ipdisk/ alltables.txt

This information can be used to determine business cycles for your industry and others, which should also dictate your management tactics. It can also be used to compare your company sales with industry trends. If your sales trends do nothing more than mirror the industry trends, then your sales staff is average. If your sales trends exceed the industry, then your sales staff is above average; and if your sales trends are lower than the industry trends, then your sales staff is below average.

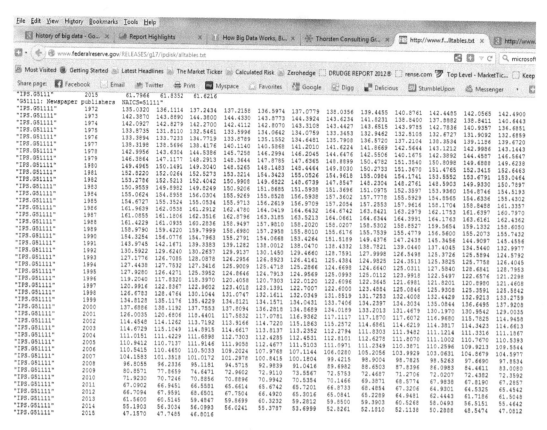

So, how could Big Data have been used by the newspaper industry to identify its downward (and continuing downward) trend quickly? This information should have persuaded management teams to restructure, diversify, or abandon the newspaper industry years ago. The next analysis was performed using the IPS data for newspaper publishers and copied into Excel. Then, a chart was created to look at the industry as a whole.

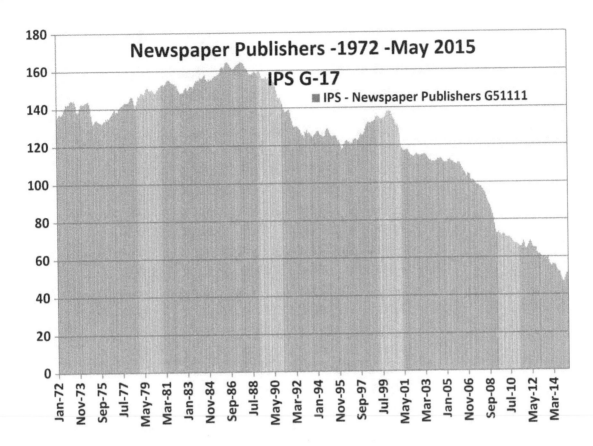

Note the peak around 1986–87. This was the timeframe when personal computers became more prevalent. The trend for users to start accessing news information online was just over the horizon.

How can we use this information to understand business cycles and trends in sales revenue? The Excel data were used to create 3- and 12-month averages.

	Y	Z	AA	AB	AC	AD
1130		IPS	3 mo avg	12 mo avg	3 mo Trail	12 mo trail
1131	2013	61.56	61.59447	64.88683	0.939436	0.979591
1132		60.5145	61.1931	64.26645	0.917334	0.968989
1133		59.4847	60.51973	63.50267	0.892979	0.954963
1134		59.8699	59.95637	62.84596	0.88016	0.942619
1135		60.3232	59.8926	62.33189	0.885581	0.933954
1136		59.2812	59.82477	61.83019	0.899422	0.926921
1137		59.85	59.81813	61.39402	0.911502	0.922444
1138		59.3903	59.50717	60.90747	0.912618	0.918881
1139		60.5268	59.92237	60.53903	0.92065	0.916054
1140		58.0493	59.32213	60.17278	0.923919	0.913376
1141		56.5151	58.36373	59.73915	0.925865	0.910033
1142		55.4642	56.6762	59.23577	0.915768	0.906911
1143	2014	55.1903	55.7232	58.70496	0.904679	0.904728
1144		56.3034	55.65263	58.35403	0.909459	0.908002
1145		56.0993	55.86433	58.07192	0.923076	0.91448
1146		56.0241	56.14227	57.75143	0.936385	0.918936
1147		55.3787	55.83403	57.33939	0.932236	0.919905
1148		53.6999	55.03423	56.87428	0.919924	0.919846
1149		52.8261	53.96823	56.28896	0.902205	0.916848
1150		52.181	52.90233	55.68818	0.889008	0.914308
1151		52.1138	52.37363	54.9871	0.874025	0.908292
1152		50.2888	51.52787	54.34039	0.868611	0.903073
1153		48.5474	50.31667	53.67642	0.862122	0.898513
1154		47.0812	48.63913	52.97783	0.858193	0.894355
1155	2015	47.157	47.5952	52.30839	0.854136	0.891039
1156		48.6079	47.61537	51.6671	0.855582	0.885408
1157		49.8802	48.54837	51.14884	0.86904	0.880784
1158		51.2855	49.92453	50.75396	0.88925	0.878835
1159		51.3863	50.85067	50.42126	0.910747	0.879348

Charting out the IPS, 3- and 12-month averages produce the following graph. Note the continuous decline which is almost always below the 12-month average. The newspapers have continued their decline since the beginning of the 21st century.

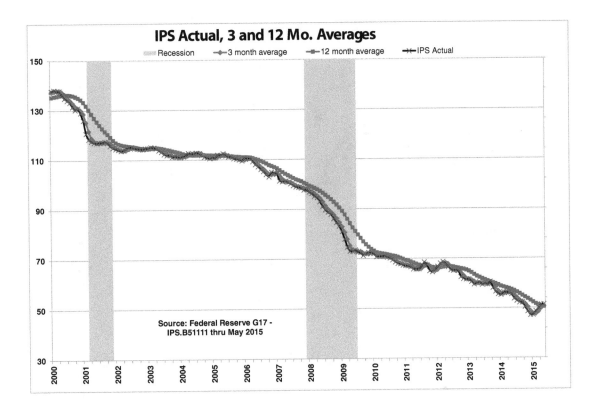

IPS Actual, 3 and 12 Mo. Averages

Source: Federal Reserve G17 -
IPS.B51111 thru May 2015

Graph the trailing averages. It is easy to see when the data fall below 1.0. Any time the data are below 1.0, the industry is declining. A prudent management team should be taking recessionary steps. When the data climb above 1.0, the industry is growing, and the management team should be concerned with expansionary actions. Unfortunately, reviewing the data with the calculations and reviewing the preceding charts, it is clear that the newspaper industry has been in continuous decline.

KNOWLEDGE CHECK

6. Where do the Industrial Production Statistics come from?

    a. The U.S. Census.
    b. The Bureau of Labor and Statistics.
    c. The Federal Reserve.
    d. U.S. Small Business Administration.

7. What was the industry code for newspaper publishers?

    a. 51111.
    b. 50001.
    c. 54111.
    d. 44111.

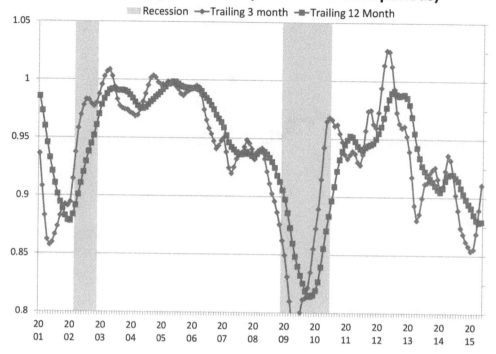

IPS Trailing 12 months (3- and 12-month periods)

Census Data

What are some other sources of Big Data to consider using for an organization?

The U.S. Census prepares the estimate of Monthly Retail Sales from 1992 through the present. The website is www.census.gov/ retail/ index.html

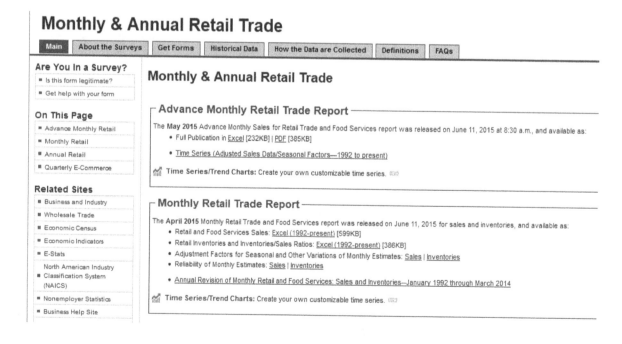

Following is an example of the data provided by the U.S. Census. The spreadsheet contains monthly data back to 1992 and also associates the industry with the North American Industry Classification System code. It would be possible to connect this data to the IPS data from the previous example.

Estimates of Monthly Retail and Food Services Sales by Kind of Business: 2014

[Estimates are shown in millions of dollars and are based on data from the Monthly Retail Trade Survey, Annual Retail Trade Survey, and administrative records]

NAICS Code	Kind of Business	Jan. 2014	Feb. 2014	Mar. 2014	Apr. 2014	May 2014	Jun. 2014	Jul. 2014	Aug. 2014	Sep. 2014	Oct. 2014	Nov. 2014	Dec. 2014	TOTAL
	NOT ADJUSTED													
	Retail and food services sales, total	383,459	380,246	432,827	431,335	458,705	433,388	443,153	450,365	420,516	437,277	437,196	499,976	5,208,443
	Retail sales and food services excl motor vehicle and parts	312,448	304,556	341,407	342,380	364,347	345,578	350,695	356,572	335,829	351,578	357,040	412,103	4,174,533
	Retail sales, total	340,554	337,371	383,428	383,622	407,633	385,525	394,494	400,267	373,426	387,116	389,581	449,272	4,632,289
	Retail sales, total (excl. motor vehicle and parts dealers)	269,543	261,681	292,008	294,667	313,275	297,715	302,036	306,474	288,739	301,417	309,425	361,399	3,598,379
	GAFO(1)	85,984	89,228	99,124	96,818	103,651	97,307	99,088	107,249	95,340	100,820	115,295	146,974	1,236,878
441	Motor vehicle and parts dealers	71,011	75,690	91,420	88,955	94,358	87,810	92,458	93,793	84,687	85,699	80,156	87,873	1,033,910
4411,4412	Automobile and other motor vehicle dealers	64,389	68,999	83,951	81,538	86,889	80,530	84,938	86,374	77,580	78,165	73,128	81,267	947,748
4411	Automobile dealers	61,212	65,021	78,497	75,474	80,094	74,183	78,760	81,103	72,680	73,795	69,808	77,634	888,261
44111	New car dealers	55,142	57,002	69,958	67,924	72,476	66,747	71,246	73,352	65,320	66,143	63,290	70,992	799,592
44112	Used car dealers	6,070	8,019	8,539	7,550	7,618	7,436	7,514	7,751	7,360	7,652	6,518	6,642	88,669
4413	Automotive parts, acc., and tire stores	6,622	6,691	7,469	7,417	7,469	7,280	7,520	7,419	7,107	7,534	7,028	6,606	86,162
442,443	Furniture, home furn., electronics, and appliance stores	15,086	15,082	16,475	15,217	16,359	15,760	16,521	17,110	16,712	16,654	19,624	23,713	204,313
442	Furniture and home furnishings stores	7,132	7,172	8,028	7,705	8,293	7,762	8,262	8,591	8,203	8,254	8,767	10,063	98,232
4421	Furniture stores	3,892	4,053	4,563	4,137	4,583	4,154	4,403	4,667	4,544	4,428	4,673	4,751	52,848
4422	Home furnishings stores	3,240	3,119	3,465	3,568	3,710	3,608	3,859	3,924	3,659	3,826	4,094	5,312	45,384
44221	Floor covering stores(2)	1,208	1,169	1,314	1,418	1,424	1,455	1,455	1,495	1,418	1,504	1,294	1,289	16,444
442299	All other home furnishings stores	1,924	1,840	2,024	2,011	2,156	2,022	2,265	2,289	2,108	2,192	2,672	3,909	27,412
443	Electronics and appliance stores	7,954	7,910	8,447	7,512	7,998	8,259	8,519	8,509	8,400	10,857	13,650	106,081	
44311	Appl.,TV, and other elect. stores	5,451	5,571	5,984	5,450	5,846	5,784	6,050	6,245	6,053	5,953	7,581	9,314	75,282
443111	Household appliance stores	1,234	1,244	1,365	1,252	1,394	1,390	1,419	1,403	1,388	1,399	1,541	1,572	16,601
443112	Radio, T.V., and other elect. stores	4,217	4,327	4,619	4,198	4,452	4,394	4,631	4,842	4,665	4,554	6,040	7,742	58,681
44312	Computer and software stores	(S)	(S)	(S)	(S)	(S)	(S)	(S)	(S)	(S)	(S)	(S)	(S)	
444	Building mat. and garden equip. and supplies dealers	19,955	19,041	24,422	30,564	33,889	30,506	29,078	26,852	26,617	27,808	25,346	24,613	318,690
4441	Building mat. and supplies dealers	17,726	16,867	20,782	24,646	27,377	25,657	25,600	23,866	23,737	24,398	22,044	21,171	273,871
44412	Paint and wallpaper stores	624	615	789	886	950	958	1,025	962	943	926	707	682	10,067
44413	Hardware stores	1,654	1,560	1,856	1,959	2,175	2,017	1,995	1,934	1,898	2,067	1,922	1,931	22,968
445	Food and beverage stores	53,828	49,656	53,925	53,697	57,208	54,676	56,680	56,553	53,633	56,122	56,263	60,610	662,853
4451	Grocery stores	48,871	44,738	48,522	48,141	51,084	48,726	50,568	50,468	48,034	50,183	50,178	52,109	591,622
44511	Supermarkets and other grocery (except convenience) stores	47,167	43,070	46,679	46,278	49,079	46,766	48,510	48,396	46,133	48,304	48,391	50,366	569,139
4453	Beer, wine, and liquor stores	3,396	3,372	3,697	3,713	4,202	4,098	4,249	4,223	3,861	4,092	4,137	5,610	48,650
446	Health and personal care stores	24,385	22,997	24,863	24,658	25,398	24,669	25,053	25,107	25,077	25,971	24,518	29,448	302,144
44611	Pharmacies and drug stores	20,712	19,203	20,544	20,682	21,118	20,488	20,980	20,707	20,785	21,765	20,285	24,137	251,406
447	Gasoline stations	42,164	40,152	45,742	46,630	49,803	48,322	49,438	48,302	45,062	44,942	39,730	36,515	536,802
448	Clothing and clothing access. stores	15,070	17,427	19,968	20,217	21,451	18,829	19,700	21,855	18,564	20,117	23,300	32,350	248,848

2015 / 2014 / 2013 / 2012 / 2011 / 2010 / 2009 / 2008 / 2007 / 2006 / 2005 / 2004 / 2003 / 2002 / 2001 / 2000 / 1999 / 1998 / 1997 / 1996 / 1995 / 1994 / 1993 / 1992

DATABASE TOOLS

Your data or analysis will be limited if you do not access good prediction software. To complement your spreadsheet analysis, consider acquiring Crystal Ball (www.oracle.com/ technetwork/ middleware / crystalball/ overview/ index.html) or @ Risk (www.palisade.com/ risk/), which are Excel add-ins that perform Monte Carlo simulation analysis. In addition, Domo (www.domo.com) is a new business management platform that brings all business platforms together combining B.I., predictive analytics and Big Data.

The first add-in, @RISK (pronounced "at risk,") performs risk analysis using a Monte Carlo simulation to show many possible outcomes in the spreadsheet model—and tells how likely they are to occur. It mathematically and objectively computes and tracks many different possible future scenarios, then identifies the probabilities and risks associated with each different scenario. This means users can judge which risks to take and which ones to avoid, allowing for the best decision making under uncertainty.

@ RISK also helps plan the best risk management strategies through the integration of RISKOptimizer, which combines Monte Carlo simulation with the latest solving technology to optimize any spreadsheet with uncertain values. Using genetic algorithms[3] or OptQuest, along with @ RISK functions, RISKOptimizer can determine the best allocation of resources, the optimal asset allocation, the most efficient schedule, and much more.[4]

Oracle Crystal Ball is the leading spreadsheet-based application for predictive modeling, forecasting, simulation, and optimization. It gives unparalleled insight into the critical factors affecting risk. With Crystal Ball, users make the right tactical decisions to reach the objectives and gain a competitive edge under even the most uncertain market conditions.[5]

According to Domo's website, "To do the job well, users need the right information at the right time. Unfortunately, that information lives in an ever-increasing mess of disconnected spreadsheets, systems, databases, and applications."[6]

Domo solves that problem by bringing a business and its data together in one intuitive platform. With Domo, users can create dashboards to put all of their information in one place and use it to make faster, better-informed decisions.

---

[3] Note: A genetic algorithm (GA) is a method for solving both constrained and unconstrained optimization problems based on a natural selection process that mimics biological evolution. The algorithm repeatedly modifies a population of individual solutions. At each step, the genetic algorithm randomly selects individuals from the current population and uses them as parents to produce the children for the next generation. Over successive generations, the population "evolves" toward an optimal solution. https:/ / www.mathworks.com/ discovery/ genetic-algorithm.html

[4] "@Risk," Statistics.com, www.statistics.com/ software-directory/ risk-spreadsheet-add-in/ , Accessed 3/ 30/ 17

[5] www.oracle.com/ technetwork/ middleware/ crystalball/ overview/ index.html, Accessed 3/ 30/ 17

[6] https:/ / www.domo.com/ company/ what-is-domo, Accessed 3/ 30/ 17

KNOWLEDGE CHECK

8. The monthly retail sales data can be obtained from

    a. The U.S. Census.
    b. Bureau of Labor and Statistics.
    c. The Federal Reserve.
    d. U.S. Small Business Administration.

BIG DATA VISUALIZATION

What is Big Data visualization? According to SAS:[7]

> Data visualization is the presentation of data in a pictorial or graphical format. For centuries, people have depended on visual representations such as charts and maps to understand information more easily and quickly.

> As more and more data are collected and analyzed, decision makers at all levels welcome data visualization software that enables them to see analytical results presented visually, find relevance among the millions of variables, communicate concepts and hypotheses to others, and even predict the future.

> Because of the way the human brain processes information, it is faster for people to grasp the meaning of many data points when they are displayed in charts and graphs rather than poring over piles of spreadsheets or reading pages and pages of reports.

Text Analytics[8]

Text analytics is the process of deriving high-quality information from text. Insights are derived from understanding patterns and trends through statistical pattern learning. Text mining requires structuring the input text, identifying patterns within the structured data, and finally interpreting the output. Text mining includes text categorization, text clustering, concept or entity extraction, production of granular taxonomies, sentiment analysis, document summarization, and entity relation modeling (that is, learning relations between named entities). The goal of text mining is to transform text into data by use of natural language processing and analytical methods. One example is to scan a set of documents written in a natural language for predictive classification purposes or populate a database with the extracted information.

- Named entities extraction: Helps answer the questions: "who, what, and where?"
- Document summarization: The creation of a shortened version of a text by a computer program.
- Theme extraction: Answers the question: "What are the important words being used?"
- Concept extraction: Answers the question: "What are the important high-level concepts?"
- Sentiment analysis: Answers the question: "Is what's being said 'positive' or 'negative'?

---

[7] "Data Visualization: What It Is and Why It Matters," SAS, www.sas.com/ en_us/ insights/ big-data/ data-visualization.html

[8] Rao, Venky, "An Introduction to Text Analytics," accessed March 21, 2016, Data Science Central, www.datasciencecentral.com/

Practice Questions

1. List some of the determinants of pricing.

2. Describe the Big Data accessed from Best Buy.

3. List several sources of Big Data that can be compared to your organization.

4. Describe what text analytics is.

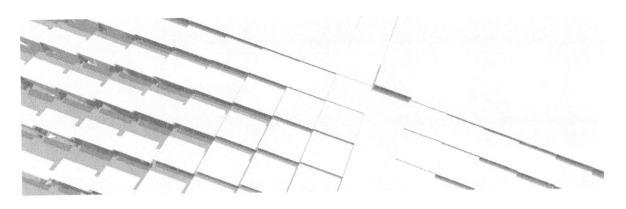

Chapter 7

EXAMPLES OF BIG DATA

LEARNING OBJECTIVES

After completing this chapter, you should be able to do the following:

- Identify how companies are currently using Big Data.
- Distinguish how organizations can apply the Big Data examples in the chapter to their organizations.

INTRODUCTION

The year 2016 was the year that Big Data was no longer a buzzword. Technology and the capacity to manage data have caught up to the point that everyone can now use Big Data—not just the early adopters.[1]

This year, 2017, will see an increase in data mining and collection and an ever-increasing amount of data that can be tailored to specific tasks. There will also be increased risk of data breaches. Established and emerging companies are using data to inform decision making, drive customer engagement, close sales, predict spending patterns, and increase revenue.

Additionally, machine learning and artificial intelligence will be key players in data analysis. Forbes predicts an increase in CDO (Chief Data Officers), analysists, programmers, and specialists with Big Data knowledge, though they see the demand for Big Data staffing tapering off as infrastructure and machines become adjusted to the new data load.[2]

---

[1] www.kdnuggets.com/ 2016/ 12/ big-data-main-developments-2016-key-trends-2017.html

[2] https:/ / www.forbes.com/ sites/ bernardmarr/ 2016/ 03/ 15/ 17-predictions-about-the-future-of-big-data-everyone-should-read/ # 191159f71a32

The focus will be on fine-tuning big data into more manageable information, such as "fast data" and "actionable data" to cut down on the extra noise that some companies are getting overwhelmed by when they ask the wrong questions of their data.[3]

This chapter includes examples of how Big Data is being created and used by businesses. The goal of this chapter is to understand (through the examples provided) that there are many types of data that an organization has access to, or can obtain access to, that allow increased insights into their business. The reader should view each example as a potential application for their organization.

The purpose is not to overwhelm but to review a myriad of examples to heighten the reader's awareness of the many different applications of Big Data and to trigger thoughts about how Big Data may be applied in your company.

EXAMPLES OF BIG DATA

Uber

Uber uses Big Data to know customers' every move. Where they live, where they eat, where they work, where they travel, and the timing of these activities. Uber has partnered with "Starwood Preferred Guest," which is an elite club that allows you to earn points whenever you use Uber. The catch is you allow Uber and Starwood to use your data however they see fit.[4]

The picture reads "By clicking allow, you agree to give Starwood Preferred Guest: Access to your full name, email, photo, and promo code. Access to all of your Uber activity. This includes all pickup and drop-off locations and times, fare amount, distances traveled, and Uber products used. Starwood Preferred Guest will use this information according to its Privacy Policy."

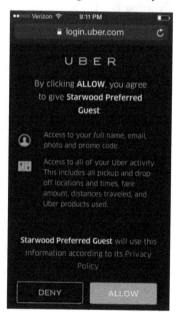

---

[3] www.smartdatacollective.com/ tonyshan/ 309691/ big-data-really-dead

[4] https:/ / www.forbes.com/ sites/ ronhirson/ 2015/ 03/ 23/ uber-the-big-data-company/ # bde68b018c7f, Accessed 3/ 30/ 17

Halo Top

The light ice cream brand is taking the frozen treat sector by storm, at a time when most brands are struggling to keep their market share. They've completely ignored traditional marketing routes, and use Big Data provided by Facebook, Twitter, and Instagram to place specific ads and closely monitor their return on investment for these digital ads. Mr. Woolverton, the founder of Halo Top, said, "You can make $100 go a lot further through a Facebook ad where you can target demographically, psychographically, geographically, et cetera, than by taking out ad space in a newspaper. If you can focus on people who actually want to see your ads, everyone is happier." Halo Top's sales have increased 2,500 percent from 2015 to 2016.[5]

Electronic Arts

There are more than 2 billion video game players on the planet, and the $20 billion-dollar industry leads in many categories. Electronic Arts has one of the largest market shares, and they use big data to ensure customer engagement throughout the gaming experience. For example, games that are too difficult on beginning levels, or too easy on advanced levels, cause players to quit, and this hampers a videogame's success. Electronic Arts looks at where they lose players during game play, sees if there are bottlenecks that are causing players to quit, and uses this information to tailor new games going forward.[6]

NFL

The NFL is using Big Data to track players on the field for multiple purposes—specifically free agency. Using two sensors, one in each shoulder pad, and a refined GPS-like tracking system on two levels of the stadium, the NFL can now track player mileage. Some general managers see this as a way to look at free agency—to judge how much a veteran has put on his body, like injuries, miles, acceleration, deceleration, and so on. "With enough good data, coaches and trainers could more finely tune training sessions for different personnel groups, essentially personalizing practice around the different kinds of needs of, say, nose tackles versus wide receivers."[7]

Williams-Sonoma

By using and refining search optimization and targeted email messaging based on users' search histories, Williams-Sonoma increased revenue by more than $1 million in three months. Data is involved in every level of decision-making in the company, like algorithmically driven site search to provide more relevant and personalized search. According to Sameer Hassan, Williams-Sonoma's vice president of e-commerce and marketing technology, "AH retail is going to be dependent on our ability to give customers a much more relevant experience."[8]

eCare21

Using data analytics to track thousands of pieces of health data through Fitbits, smartphones, physical activity monitors, and other easily accessible technology, eCare21 monitors senior citizens that have trouble accessing traditional healthcare. The information is put together in a dashboard so that family,

---

[5] http://adage.com/article/print-edition/halo-top-conquering-ice-cream-biz-ads/308177/, Accessed 3/30/17

[6] https://datafloq.com/read/gaming-industry-turns-big-data-improve-gaming-expe/137, Accessed 3/30/17

[7] "The NFL Is Finally Tapping Into the Power of Data," *Wired*, https://www.wired.com/2016/01/the-nfls-impending-data-revolution/, Accessed 3/30/17.

[8] www.mytotalretail.com/video/single/how-williams-sonoma-is-using-big-data-to-drive-decision-making/, Accessed 3/30/17

caregivers, and doctors can get a full picture of the senior's health without ever seeing them. Shortages in the healthcare community can be alleviated by similar services that also integrate telehealth services. "According to the National Business Group on Health, nine in 10 large employers will provide telehealth services to their employees in 2017. By 2019, NBG predicts, this number will leap to 97%."[9]

Ford

Ford is using Big Data to extend their impact on their products. Instead of ending the cycle when the vehicle leaves the factory, Ford can now monitor what items need repair or replacement when they are serviced at the local Ford dealership and see what components break down most easily. Ford can also use this information to re-engineer failing pieces with more durability.[10]

Heineken

Heineken uses Big Data to track sales as they correspond with weather reports to see where they sell best in regions during different seasons, weather patterns, and so on, so they can always have their beer in the right place at the right time. They are also testing a program called Shopperception, which is based on Xbox Kinect sensors, to see exactly when customers are buying beer, what their behaviors are in front of the shelf, and getting real-time purchase information. This gives them a way to see exactly how their beer is being purchased, where in the store it is being purchased, and when.[11]

Marist College

Marist College has developed an analytical model that can predict with 75 percent accuracy which students will succeed and which will fail based on the first two weeks of course work. Marist College has used this model to increase degree completion rates. The use of this model raises a lot of ethical questions, but so far it has been used for a positive purpose.[12]

Taco Bell

Taco Bell uses Big Data to stay in tune with customer experience. Taco Bell has a division they nicknamed the "Fishbowl," which listens to and gathers all the information about its company on Facebook, Instagram, Twitter, and the like. The executives across the company come together for 15 minutes every morning to get a report from the Fishbowl to see in real time how the company is doing. For example, when Taco Bell rolled out breakfast, the East Coast stores had miscalculated the demand, resulting in very long lines, which were broadcast all over social media. By the time the Midwest and West Coast stores were opening that same day, the problem had been resolved, and there were no wait times.[13]

Sensors—Consumer Health and Safety

The advent of sensors inside or attached to devices is changing the way we experience many activities, from sports to monitoring our health. For example, Fitbit is a tracker worn on the wrist that records

---

[9] https://www.forbes.com/sites/mikemontgomery/2016/10/26/the-future-of-health-care-is-in-data-analytics/#2bd701f23ee2, Accessed 3/30/17

[10] https://www.forbes.com/sites/joannmuller/2015/10/22/how-ford-is-using-big-data-to-change-the-way-we-use-our-cars/#557df6d83d2d, Accessed 3/30/17

[11] https://datafloq.com/read/how-heineken-interacts-with-customers-using-big-da/384, Accessed 3/30/17

[12] www.businessinsider.com/how-colleges-use-big-data-2016-6, Accessed 3/30/17

[13] https://www.getvenga.com/news/2016/5/23/restaurant-operators-make-big-data-small, Accessed 3/30/17

steps, distance, calories burned, and active minutes. The Fitbit has a wireless connection to the wearer's computer system.

At the Consumer Electronics Show in Las Vegas, manufacturers displayed chips to improve an individual's posture and sensors in sports equipment (including basketballs, golf clubs, and tennis balls) to help train smarter. There is even a sensor to handle mundane but important tasks such as locating lost keys.

Another application of this technology is specialty carpets containing sensors that can keep seniors alive and independent longer by identifying normal walking patterns. These carpets can notice when a person's gait begins to change, possibly predicting a fall. Falls are one of the major events that result in senior citizens relocating from their residences to senior living centers. Also, broken hips resulting from falls may be the onset of the end of a person's life. Fitness devices have also been used to identify areas of natural disasters such as earthquakes. Personal fitness tracker Jawbone reported that users woke suddenly in areas close to the epicenter of an earthquake—Napa, Sonoma, and Vallejo—right after it struck. In areas further away, like Modesto and Santa Cruz, fewer users were disturbed. This is a powerful demonstration of how Big Data can allow anyone from emergency relief workers to governments to measure the effects of a disaster.[14]

KNOWLEDGE CHECK

1. Which of the following was listed as a sensor?

    a. A sensor to advise an owner when a pet wants to come in.
    b. A sensor to notify you that mail has arrived in your mailbox.
    c. A sensor to find your keys.
    d. A sensor to detect someone at your front door.

Call Centers—Displeased Customers

United Healthcare Services Inc. is gaining insight from Big Data by investigating customer speech patterns in data call centers to see whether displeasure can be identified. By noticing patterns in customer interactions, UHS can pinpoint situations that lead to customer turnover.[15]

Speech analytics systems can analyze tone and sentiment of voice and talk or silence patterns to gauge emotion and satisfaction and tie detection of user-defined phrases to specific agent actions—in short, identify and prioritize what needs fixing, and then contribute to the resolution.[16]

---

[14] Caitlin Dewey, "What Personal Fitness Trackers Like Jawbone Tell Us About Earthquakes, Public Health—and Just About Anything Else," *The Washington Post*, Accessed 3/ 30/ 17, www.washingtonpost.com/ news/ the-intersect/ wp/ 2014/ 08/ 25/ what-personal-fitness-trackers-like-jawbone-tell-us-about-earthquakes-public-health-and-just-about-anything-else/

[15] Nicole Laskowski, "Analytics 3.0—The Old Guard Masters How to Build Data Products," *TechTarget*, Accessed 3/ 30/ 17, searchcio.techtarget.com/ opinion/ Analytics-30-the-old-guard-masters-how-to-build-data-products

[16] Karen Schwartz, "How to Use Speech Analytics in the Call Center," *CRMSearch*, Accessed 3/ 30/ 17, www.crmsearch.com/ call-center-speech-analytics.php

Another great example of companies using Big Data is GE. GE puts devices into anything "that spins" in order to find what machines need maintenance, which processes can be curtailed, and what machines are experiencing wear and tear at greater rates. Because GE makes almost half of its income from maintenance services for those machines, it gains a huge advantage in its services business from all of that data. This results in one gas turbine's sensor producing more information in a day than all of Twitter does in a week.[17]

Weather and Flight Information—Lodging Chains

People travel less during bad weather, which results in fewer purchases of overnight lodging. However, some chains are using bad weather to their advantage. Red Roof Inn made the connection between bad weather, canceled flights, and stranded passengers. When flights were canceled due to inclement weather, passengers turned into potential and desperate customers. Red Roof Inn sourced readily available flight cancellation and weather information and used it increase bookings. The company built an algorithm, sorted based on inn and air terminal areas. This algorithm could be used to target passengers with hotel deal information. Incorporating the knowledge that travelers would be searching for hotels via their cell phones, Red Roof Inn used multiple mobile platforms to specifically target travelers searching hotel accommodations and made it as easy as possible for them to book a hotel.

Consider the impact of Big Data. Note that 1 percent to 3 percent of flights are canceled every day, which means 150 to 500 flights (in other words, 25,000 to 90,000 stranded passengers). Using Big Data to target these passengers, Red Roof Inn managed to increase its business by 10 percent from 2013 to 2014.[18]

KNOWLEDGE CHECK

2. What percentage of flights are canceled (on average) every day?

    a. 1 percent to 3 percent.
    b. 2 percent to 4 percent.
    c. 3 percent to 5 percent.
    d. 4 percent to 6 percent.

Weather Information and Power Outages—Pizza Chains

Pizza chains also use weather to target potential customers. One pizza chain delivers coupons based on severe weather and power outages. The business understands that people will be unable to cook when the power is out, and thus targets these individual with mobile ad campaigns to entice them to purchase pizza. The targeted marketing campaign has a 20 percent response rate, which is higher than the national average.[19]

---

[17] Laskowski.

[18] Chuck Schaeffer, "5 Retail Big Data Examples," *CRMSearch*, Accessed 3/ 30/ 17, www.crmsearch.com/ retail-big-data.php

[19] Ibid.

Field Sensors—John Deere

Agribusiness pioneer John Deere is making waves in the industry with Big Data. The John Deere Field Connect system screens dampness levels and sends the information over a wireless connection for farmers to see. The natural sensors likewise gauge "air and soil temperature, wind speed, humidity, solar, radiation, and precipitation and leaf wetness."

The information will help farmers to know when crops are approaching ideal moisture levels. Equipped with this data, ranchers can settle on watering system choices. Pattern information can likewise demonstrate how much the season influences moisture retention.[20]

Social Networks—EMI

Record company EMI uses Big Data to predict future music trends. EMI pays close attention to how music purchasers are consuming newly released music. For example, EMI looks at how the music is being referenced on social media networks, as well as how it is being played on streaming services. The company then analyzes the data and breaks it down by location, demographics, and subcultures and assists the music distributor to deliver pinpoint advertising and forecast product demand with a high confidence level. This concept is applicable to other retailers who can also aggregate feeds from social networks to build an understanding of how new products will be received by new or existing markets, or even how their products and company reputation are perceived among the public.[21]

eBureau—Financial Services

After new customer acquisitions had hit an all-time low, a financial services firm sought to use Big Data as a means to identify which new clients would evolve into the most worthwhile investment opportunities. The organization supplemented its client demographic information with outsider information acquired from eBureau. Sales lead opportunities were fortified with other consumer information including incomes, ages, occupations and related factors. The improved data set is then entered into an algorithm which recognizes which new customer leads ought to get extra attention and which should be passed over. Using Big Data has resulted in an 11 percent increase in new customer win rates. Simultaneously, the firm has brought down deals related costs by 14.5 percent.[22]

KNOWLEDGE CHECK

3. EMI partially obtains music trends from

   a. YouTube.
   b. Google.
   c. Social media networks.
   d. Instagram.

---

[20] Conner Forrest, "Ten Examples of IoT and Big Data Working Well Together, *ZDNet*, Accessed 3/ 30/ 17, www.zdnet.com/ article/ ten-examples-of-iot-and-big-data-working-well-together/
[21] Schaeffer.
[22] Ibid.

One retail Big Data example that merits special attention is Target's pregnancy detection. Target correlated baby shower registry information with its Guest ID program so as to discern when a customer is likely to be pregnant. Target's Guest ID is a unique customer ID that tracks buying history, credit card use, survey responses, customer support interactions, email click-throughs, and website visits. The organization supplements the shopper activities with demographic information like age, ethnicity, instruction, conjugal status, the number of children, assessed salary, work history, and life events (such as divorces, filing for bankruptcy, or moves).

By looking at customers who registered on the baby shower registry with the purchasing history from their Guest ID, the retailer could follow changes in shopping tendencies as the customer advanced throughout her pregnancy. For instance, during the initial 20 weeks, pregnant women started acquiring supplements like calcium, magnesium, and zinc. In the second trimester, they started purchasing bigger pants and larger amounts of hand sanitizers, unscented salve, scent-free cleanser, and enormous packs of cotton balls. Altogether, the retailer could pinpoint around 25 items pregnant women purchased throughout their pregnancies.

By applying these buying practices to all customers, Target had the capacity to recognize when customers were pregnant despite the fact that they had not directly notified Target or anyone else. Target then forecast every shopper's likelihood of being pregnant with a pregnancy-prediction model. With this model, Target assigned customers with a score that rated their likelihood of being pregnant. These numbers were used to identify the specific pregnant segment, which then received targeted promotions aimed at each step of the pregnancy. These customers did not stop at purchasing items for their infants. Their purchasing behaviors as a whole were heightened. From using Big Data, Target increased its income from $44 billion in 2002 to $67 billion in 2010. Though the retailer did not freely remark on this program, Target's CEO is on record telling financial specialists that the organization's "heightened focus on items and categories that appeal to specific guest segments such as mom and baby" significantly added to the retailer's success.[23]

Despite the customer security and advertising considerations which must be questioned, this is an important lesson for retailers.

KNOWLEDGE CHECK

4. Target is known for a Big Data trend identifier. What trend does Target believe that it can predict?

    a. Marriage.
    b. Pregnancy.
    c. Illness.
    d. Divorce.

---

[23] Ibid.

Hadoop—Morgan Stanley

Morgan Stanley took a lesson from Target's book and tried to follow suit. "We dumped every log we could get, including the web and all the different database logs, put them into Hadoop and ran time-based correlations," says Gary Bhattacharjee, executive director of enterprise information management.[24] The firm was then able to see market activity and how it corresponded with web issues and database read-write problems.

At the point when Morgan attempted to do some portfolio investigation, it found that conventional databases and grid computing wouldn't scale to the vast volumes of information that its information researchers needed. The IT office connected 15 old servers using Hadoop. As opposed to working with smaller sets of data, Hadoop allowed the bank to work with vast volumes of information from a multitude of angles. It allowed Morgan Stanley to bring cheap infrastructure into a framework, install Hadoop, and let it run. The company now has a very scalable solution for portfolio analysis.

Automotive Data Generator—Ford Fusion

Ford has a large, fragmented environment from which to acquire Big Data. On top of that, Ford has invested heavily in creating more connected machines, including their cars. For instance, Ford's current hybrid Fusion model produces up to 25 gigabytes of data every hour. This information is a potential goldmine for Ford provided they can extract knowledge from the information.

Ford had been pushing to adopt Big Data technologies for around a year. The company's IT group has been able to get a high-level view of all the data sources and the complex analytics puzzle that bridge across the whole organization. This effort and the need to process information in new ways were driving forces for IT in selecting Hadoop.[25]

Internet—Virgin Atlantic

Virgin Atlantic has connected numerous Boeing 787 airplanes and cargo devices via the Internet. Every plane has numerous connected parts producing an extensive volume of information.

Every associated flight can deliver more than half a terabyte of data. The information could be used to anticipate maintenance issues or to enhance flight and fuel effectiveness. Unfortunately, Virgin Atlantic reported that it has not been able to make much use out of all this data. Trials with Hadoop did not generate the insights needed; therefore, the company had to look at other software vendors.[26]

Industrial Internet—GE

GE has invested heavily in Big Data as seen in the previous machine services example—from harnessing trains and planes to power the Internet and beyond. General Electric is best known for its machine making, yet it has begun marketing itself as a major information organization as well by pushing its vision for an "Industrial Internet"—the idea that machines ought to be associated with the web to build productivity and decrease downtime. In 2012, it dispatched programming to help carriers and railways

---

[24] Tom Groenfeldt, "Morgan Stanley Takes On Big Data With Hadoop," *Forbes*, Accessed 3/ 30/ 17, www.forbes.com/ sites/ tomgroenfeldt/ 2012/ 05/ 30/ morgan-stanley-takes-on-big-data-with-hadoop/
[25] Nicole Hemsoth, "How Ford Is Putting Hadoop Pedal to the Metal," *Datanami*, Accessed 3/ 30/ 17, www.datanami.com/ 2013/ 03/ 16/ how_ford_is_putting_hadoop_pedal_to_the_metal/
[26] Matthew Finnegan, "Boeing 787s to Create Half a Terabyte of Data Per Flight, says Virgin Atlantic," *Computer World UK*, Accessed 3/ 30/ 17, www.computerworlduk.com/ news/ data/ boeing-787s-create-half-terabyte-of-data-per-flight-says-virgin-atlantic-3433595/

move their information to the cloud and joined forces with Accenture to shape Taleris, a startup that will help the air industry foresee mechanical problems and decrease flight delays or cancellations.[27]

Manufacturing Equipment—TempuTech

TempuTech's Big Data framework is having an impact on the agribusiness business. The organization offers connected systems that screen ideal grain inventory and identify potential hazards (in other words, grain elevators) in systems.

Dangers, such as broken belts or bearings, can be observed. Grain management systems can track the moisture and temperature of grain bins, permitting air circulation, and fan settings to be manually adjusted to allow for changes. This information is additionally sent to farm operators, who can use it to anticipate dampness and temperature changes taking into account changes in weather.[28]

Automated Food Production—King's Hawaiian

King's Hawaiian Bread Processing Plants partnered with Rockwell Automation to build a highly automated bread-baking facility with specialized machines. The employees have an additional tool to screen bread production and can monitor operations from anywhere via the Internet. The information gathered permitted the organization to decrease potential downtime of machines and lower maintenance costs.[29]

KNOWLEDGE CHECK

5. TempuTech was being used in which aspect of agribusiness Big Data?

    a. Grain elevators.
    b. Combines.
    c. John Deere tractors.
    d. Fertilizer spreaders.

Logistic sensors—UPS

UPS uses sensor information and Big Data analytics to save money, increase efficiency, and reduce its environmental impact. The vehicle sensors screen speed, miles per gallon, mileage, the number of stops, and motor engine health. The sensors catch more than 200 data points for every vehicle in the 80,000 fleet every single day. As a result of this data idling time, fuel consumption, and harmful emissions are reduced.

UPS also uses On-Road Integrated Optimization and Navigation (ORION) to optimize delivery routes. ORION optimizes the routes using hundreds of millions of location data points.[30]

---

[27] Andrew Nusca, "GE unwraps 'Industrial Internet': M2M for planes, trains, manufacturing," *ZDNet*, Accessed 3/ 30/ 17, www.zdnet.com/ article/ ge-unwraps-industrial-internet-m2m-for-planes-trains-manufacturing/
[28] Doug Henschen, "GE Powers Internet of Agriculture," *Information Week*, Accessed 3/ 30/ 17, www.informationweek.com/ big-data/ software-platforms/ ge-powers-internet-of-agriculture/ d/ d-id/ 1306646
[29] Forrest.
[30] Forrest.

Data Analytics—Big Box Stores

Walmart is performing data analytics on customer and transaction information from 10 sites. Sears and Kmart are attempting to enhance the personalization of promotional campaigns, coupons, and offers with Big Data to contend better with Walmart, Target, and Amazon. As the pioneer in the space, Amazon uses 1 million Hadoop clusters to bolster its affiliate network, risk management, machine learning, and website updates.[31]

Data Analysis—Video Games

The video game industry is using Big Data to follow gameplay, anticipate distribution patterns, and break down more than 500GB of organized information and 4 TB of operational logs every day.

One side effect of the growth in the industry is an increase in the amount of data generated from video games. Video game data comes from several sources: gameplay data, micro-transactions, time stamps, social media, price points, payment systems, in-game advertising, virtual goods, multiplayer interactions, real-time events and content updates, to name a few.

To analyze the massive amount of structured and unstructured data that's generated every day by the nearly 2 billion users of video games, companies are using a variety of tools such as Hadoop. Big Data allows video game publishers to track a player's progress and activity to recogni2e any bottlenecks or trouble spots in games. This information can be used to improve many aspects of a gamer's experience, including reevaluating certain aspects of a game, so that frustrated gamers don't quit.

Supercomputers and genome databases—Icahn School of Medicine at Mount Sinai

Mount Sinai is also important in the Big Data world for embracing data scientists and supercomputers to build the future hospital. The New York City medical center is recruiting top Silicon Valley talent to build a facility that will predict diseases based on patients' genomes. This will allow the hospital to anticipate sicknesses, diminish the quantity of normal doctor's facility visits, and streamline electronic therapeutic records. At the heart of Mount Sinai's endeavors are a $3 million supercomputer named Minerva, which rapidly forms gigabytes of well-being information, and BioMe, a database of genomic examples from more than 25,000 patients.[32]

Customer Databases—Banking

The banking industry is pursuing Big Data as well. JPMorgan Chase creates significant amounts of credit card information and other value-based information about U.S. shoppers. Eventually, the bank consolidated that database, which incorporated 1.5 billion bits of data, with freely accessible economic stats from the U.S. government. Chase used new analytics to understand customer buying patterns and insights and offered those reports to the bank's customers. The innovation permitted the bank to segment its Visa Card customers into smaller segments in short amounts of time. It could then investigate customer retention patterns within those segments.

---

[31] Stacey Higginbotham, "WalmartLabs Is Building Big Data Tools—and Will Then Open Source Them," *GigaOm*, Accessed 3/ 30/ 17, https:/ / gigaom.com/ 2012/ 03/ 23/ walmart-labs-is-building-big-data-tools-and-will-then-open-source-them/

[32] "The World's Top 10 Most Innovative Companies," *Fast Company*, accessed April 14, 2016, www.fastcompany.com/ most-innovative-companies/ 2014/ industry/ big-data

Citibank is another bank that is exploring different avenues regarding better approaches to offering business clients value-based information gathered from its worldwide client base, which customers can use to distinguish new trade patterns.[33]

KNOWLEDGE CHECK

6. Chase integrated credit card data with what?

    a. Economic stats from the industry.
    b. Economic stats from the U.S. government.
    c. Economic stats from associations.
    d. Drivers' license records.

Shared Information—Financial Services

Organizations are not simply using information themselves; they are welcoming others to explore and use their information.

Intuit has launched a program for developers that provides access to the following:

- More than 65 million records and 11 million users supported today.
- Financial information from more than 19,000 financial service organizations over the United States and Canada.
- Aggregate consumer and business financial account data, in addition to auto-categorized transactions.
- Secure Application Programming Interface for cost-effective, self-serve data access.
- Software Development Kits for .NET and Java to speed up development of apps.

Another example of how a financial services institution has taken advantage of access to open customer data to improve services is Crédit Agricole (CA). The French bank has created a developer program with the slogan "applications for you and by you." The CA app store is a co-creation platform that unites the bank's clients—and their application needs—and independent developers and gives the developers access to anonymized banking information. [34]

Kaggle—Big Data Competitions

Kaggle is a hosting platform for Big Data competitions. Companies and researchers post their raw data on Kaggle so that professional and amateur statisticians from all over the world can analyze it. Whoever comes up with the best predictive model or script wins a cash prize and sometimes a job at the hosting company. This crowdsourcing approach to analyzing Big Data has attracted big-name companies like Walmart, State Farm, and GE, as well as the brightest talent in the data science sphere.[35]

---

[33] Michael Hickins, "Banks Using Big Data to Discover 'New Silk Roads,'" The CIO Report, *The Wall Street Journal*, accessed March 21, 2016, blogs.wsj.com/ cio/ 2013/ 02/ 06/ banks-using-big-data-to-discover-new-silk-roads/
[34] Jennifer Belissent, "Open Data Is Notjust for Governments Anymore..." *Forrester*, Accessed 3/ 30/ 17, blogs.forrester.com/ jennifer_belissent_phd/ 13-02-21-open_data_is_not_just_for_governments_anymore
[35] Bernard Marr, "Walmart: The Big Data Skills Crisis and Recruiting Analytics Talent," *Forbes*, Accessed 3/ 30/ 17, www.forbes.com/ sites/ bernardmarr/ 2015/ 07/ 06/ walmart-the-big-data-skills-crisis-and-recruiting-analytics-talent/ # afd2401247d5

Gnip is an application program interface (API) that allows its clients to access every online social media networking stream, including Twitter, Facebook, and Disqus. Gnip's service lets clients screen and parses social networking streams by characteristics like keywords, patterns, trends, and geographical locations. In addition to being acquired by Twitter and offering access to Twitter's full authentic stream of tweets—which the Library of Congress uses—the organization also offers turnkey solutions that collect social data from up to six different sources.[36]

KNOWLEDGE CHECK

7. Gnip is designed to access Big Data in what areas?

    a. Unstructured internal email systems.

    b. Video streams only.

    c. Social media streams.

    d. Governmental databases.

Big Data—Fraud Vulnerability

The sooner that claims or transaction fraud are recognized, the sooner it can be stopped and rectified. Big Data can mask fraud, but it also may be the avenue for quicker recognition of fraudulent patterns. Much of the time, fraud is found long after it occurred, when the harm has been done, and all that is left is to minimize the damage and adjust processes to keep the fraud from recurring. Big Data platforms could use analytics to search for patterns that indicate fraud, determine which regions or locations have higher rates of fraud, and even test for network vulnerabilities.[37]

MongoDB—City of Chicago

The City of Chicago is using MongoDB to minimize crime and enhance municipal services by gathering and breaking down geospatial information in real-time from more than 30 unique divisions. For example, in a given territory, the city may assess the number of 911 calls and complaints, broken lights, stolen trash cans, liquor permits, and abandoned structures, verifying that an uptick in crime is more likely than normal. The city needs to merge structured and unstructured data, do so at scale, and conduct the analysis in-house. Eventually, the city hopes to use this data in a predictive way, to prevent crimes or safety issues before they occur. Chicago has opened its data to the public, allowing others to create new services, such as an app that alerts residents when street sweepers are coming to their location.[38]

---

[36] Janet Wagner, "Two Great Social Data Platforms: How DataSift and Gnip Stack Up," *Programmable Web,* Accessed 3/30/17, www.programmableweb.com/ news/ two-great-social-data-platforms-how-datasift-and-gnip-stack/ brief/ 2014/ 02/ 10

[37] Sarah Diamond, "How to Use Big Data to Fight Financial Fraud," *Forbes,* accessed April 15, 2016, www.forbes.com/ sites/ ibm/ 2014/ 09/ 22/ how-to-use-big-data-to-fight-financial-fraud/ # 7d1a042c2561

[38] "Chicago Uses MongoDB to Create a Smarter and Safer City," MongoDB, accessed March 21, 2016, https:/ / www.mongodb.com/ customers/ city-of-chicago

Barcelona is the annual host of the Mobile World Congress technology show and is becoming a hub of innovation itself.

The city offers savvy parking meters that work on city-wide Wi-Fi, giving residents up-to-speed reports on where to stop and permitting them to pay using their telephone. Smart bus stops give travelers ongoing updates through touch-screen panels, and a city-wide sensor system informs residents about temperature, air quality, noise level, and pedestrian activity.

Barcelona constructed a Big Data system on Microsoft Azure to process and investigates the many data points it was getting. With the information generated by the framework, the city can offer better services, for example, open transportation, plan for occasions like the La Mercé Festival all the more effectively, and better evaluate the effect of tourism.[39]

KNOWLEDGE CHECK

8. What does Barcelona offer its guests and citizens?

   a. Up-to-speed reports on where to stop.
   b. Up-to-speed information about car rentals.
   c. Up-to-speed information about dining locations and hours.
   d. Up-to-speed information on hotel accommodations.

RFID Sensors—Disney World's MagicBand

Disney World is using Big Data with their MagicBand project. MagicBand is a $1 billion investment in a wearable, sensor-loaded wristband that vacationers use to do everything from registering their inn room, purchasing their lunch, and reserving a spot for particular attractions.

Wearers use the band to "'weigh in" at specific posts by tapping it against a recipient, and it tracks their path through RFID, so Disney gathers information on guest movement all through the amusement park. Using this information, Disney can accommodate more visitors, efficiently staff rides and attractions, and better regulate inventory at highly accessed shops and eateries.[40]

Bluetooth Sensors—Alex and Ani

Alex and Ani is a jewelry store chain. It has installed Bluetooth sensors in stores that can track activity and push more customized offers to clients' telephones as they enter.

The company has also collaborated with Swirl, a technology innovation company. The application tracks clients' walking habits inside the store, like a heat map, so the organization will have the capacity to better sort out and present items to customers.[41]

---

[39] Forrest.

[40] Cliff Kuang, "Disney's $1 Billion Bet on a Magical Wristband," *Wired*, Accessed 3/ 30/ 17, www.wired.com/ 2015/ 03/ disney-magicband/

[41] Claire Swedburg, "Alex and Ani Rolls Out Swirl's Bluetooth Beacons at 40 Stores," *RFID Journal*, 3/ 30/ 17, www.rfidjournal.com/ articles/ view?11475

MongoDB—MetLife Customer Service

MetLife has more than 100 million clients and more than 100 products. Its back-office systems involve an expansive network of siloed applications that make it difficult for clients and agents to get the right data. Using MongoDB, MetLife created an application that gives a single perspective of the client, totaling client and product data from more than 70 current frameworks and making it accessible to clients and agents. Furthermore, it manufactured the application in only three months. Thus, the supplier decreased the time to determine client issues, which increased customer happiness, giving representatives a chance to cross-offer and upsell using real-time analytics.[42]

KNOWLEDGE CHECK

9. How does MetLife use Big Data?

    a. To evaluate the risk of individual customers.
    b. To cross-sell products.
    c. To evaluate risk by aggregated customer data by geographic area.
    d. To detect fraudulent transactions.

IBM's Predictive Traffic Management—Lyon, France

Anyone who has been to a big city knows that traffic congestion is a real problem. It affects the health and well-being of residents who must endure rage-inducing delays and affects the economic health of the city as well. One city in France decided to proactively manage traffic congestion using IBM's predictive traffic-management software.

Transportation department officials in Lyon, France combined real-time traffic data with advanced analytics to help proactively manage traffic congestion. That means drivers spend less time in traffic because detours can be put into place quickly, along with alternate route suggestions.

How did they do it?

- Giving cities information on how they can reroute traffic to avoid traffic jams.
- Schedule delivery trucks for a less congested time.
- Traffic managers evaluate accidents, predict outcomes and make quick decisions on how to restore traffic flow. The solution could be to adjust traffic signals to allow cars to detour quickly or posting messages to alert drivers of the accident.[43]

Evolv—Xerox Human Resources

Evolv is also an important part of Big Data for mining employee performance to help reduce turnover and minimize HR. Big Data is likewise changing the way organizations contract and deal with their workforces. Like other HR programs, Evolv helps executives better comprehend workers and employment applicants by looking at their abilities, work experience, and identities. Yet, Evolv takes it to a more profound level, crunching more than 500 million information focuses on gas costs, unemployment rates, and online networking utilization to help customers like Xerox—which has cut

---

[42] "Rethinking the Customer Experience at MetLife," *mongoDB,* Accessed 3/ 30/ 17, www.mongodb.com/ customers/ metlife

[43] "This French City Said Au Revoir to Traffic Jams," People 4 Smarter Cities, Accessed 3/ 30/ 17, people4smartercities.com/ series/ french-city-said-au-revoir-traffic-jams.

attrition by 20 percent—anticipate, for instance, when a worker is destined to leave employment. Evolv's information also offers other insights that Big Data researchers have uncovered: People with two social networking records perform much higher than those with more or less, and in numerous professions, for example, call-center work, workers with criminal records perform better than those who are squeaky clean.[44]

---

[44] Mark Feffer, "HR Moves Toward Wider Use of Predictive Analytics," *Society for Human Resource Management,* Accessed 3/ 30/ 17, www.shrm.org/ hrdisciplines/ technology/ articles/ pages/ more-hr-pros-using-predictive-analytics.aspx

Practice Questions

1. What were some of the sensors that were highlighted from the consumer electronics show?

2. It was estimated that the Ford Fusion produced how many GB of information per hour?

3. What product is Disney World using to improve the customer experience as well as the flow of traffic in the amusement park?

4. Describe the Big Data app that Lyon, France, was working on with IBM.

Chapter 8

BIG DATA IN THE ACCOUNTING DEPARTMENT

LEARNING OBJECTIVES

After completing this chapter, you should be able to do the following:

- Distinguish among Big Data concepts that apply to accounting operations.
- Identify how data analysis can be used in the accounting department.

INTRODUCTION

Now that you have a good understanding of Big Data, how should it be applied specifically to accounting concepts? Accountants are familiar with accessing and manipulating structured accounting data, such as the following:

- Account name
- Account general ledger code
- Transaction amount
- Vendor name
- SKU number

Accountants are generally not familiar with unstructured data that are contained in memo fields, miscellaneous fields not accessed by traditional reports or databases, or systems (like email) that are built with the data in an unstructured format.

Nor are accountants familiar with streaming data in all of its forms nor in retrieving the data for analysis purposes. Examples of streaming data include social media discussions and machine sensor data. Some accountants may doubt that unstructured or streaming data will have any value. However, in the expanded role of the financial function, the concept of adding value to the organization is beyond traditional financial roles. This is best illustrated with the following image:

Expanding Controller Value

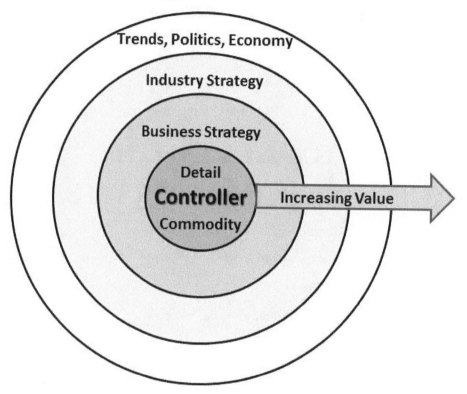

Source: Lindell, James, *Controller as Business Manager*. (AICPA, 2014).

Structured data exists at the detail or commodity level, business strategy, and industry strategy level. The industry strategy level data will most likely have to be found, downloaded, massaged and analyzed. It is possible that structured data will also exist at the broadest trend level although it will need to be manipulated in the same fashion as industry-level data.

Unstructured and streaming data can exist at all levels. It is incumbent on accountants to determine the following:

- What data are available?
- How can it be accessed?
- What tools are necessary to analyze and transform the data into useful information?

The interesting point to keep in mind is that the data that are not being accessed in structured, unstructured and streaming arenas have the potential to add significantly to the value created in the accounting department.

This chapter will illustrate methods for applying Big Data approaches to daily accounting functions as well as ways to use Big Data and data analysis for operational teams.

BIG DATA FOR THE CFO

According to Infochimps, a subsidiary of IT consulting giant Computer Sciences Corporation, Big Data is essential for today's enterprise financial strategies.

In past practices, control or compliance issues, treasury issues, and financial reporting were the primary focuses of financial executives. "Today, CFOs are expected to be strategic business partners with operating units and close confidants to the CEO."[1] Today's CFO will be involved with strategy, board issues, revenue development, cost control, and profitability, among many other tasks. On many occasions, CFOs and controllers will be required to assume additional duties in the areas of legal, human resources, and information technology. It is no surprise that the CFO's job description has changed more than any other corporate executive position.

Big Data is applicable to enterprise financial strategies more than any other innovation seen by the CFO in recent years. Big Data empowers the CFO to access and understand areas that have previously been inaccessible. This will result in the CFO getting ahead of the business' needs. Some samples of how Big Data can help the CFO include the following:

- Planning and forecasting with information-driven planning, rolling forecasts and multi-year plans overall dimensions of the business.
- Minimizing risk and fraud by constantly filtering through the points of interest of each occasion and exchange looking for the frequently inconspicuous marks of extortion or some different business risk factors.
- Advanced financial and management analytics for monthly books, statutory reporting, and variance analysis.
- Profitability modeling and optimization with cutting-edge cost analysis, product or customer viability, and allocations.
- Financial system administration with comprehensive score-carding using innovative data visualization.
- Previously impossible financial, ratio, and related information analysis that can lead to new insights, applications, and enhanced company profitability and value.

KNOWLEDGE CHECK

1. Based on the text, which statement is most accurate?

   a. Big Data is second in importance to an established culture.

   b. Big Data is second in importance only to lean management techniques.

   c. Big Data is applicable to enterprise financial strategies more than any other innovation seen by the CFO in recent years.

   d. Big Data will play an important role in seeking out wasteful practices within the organization.

---

[1] "Big Data for the CFO," Infochimps, Accessed 3/31/17, www.infochimps.com/big-data-for-cfo/

Interestingly, the CFO, CIO, and CEO can cooperate to improve corporate performance with the ability to implement Big Data arrangements rapidly and without the expenses of employing new groups of developers.

BIG DATA AREAS OF FOCUS

In the previous chapter, we looked a whole host of applications for Big Data from traffic flow management to baking better bread. The opportunities to apply Big Data analytics to accounting are similarly broad. So what are some of the specific areas where Big Data can be applied?

- Accounts receivable
- Accounts payable
- Duplicate payment detection
- Sampling
- Data imports, extractions, and analysis
- Continuous auditing and monitoring
- Fraud detection and monitoring
- Analysis of procurement cards
- Payroll and time sheets
- Joins and comparisons
- Inventory audits

We'll look at each of these areas in more depth in the sections that follow.

Accounts Receivable (AR)

According to Ventana Research, Big Data applications can be used in accounts receivable to advance consumer satisfaction and loyalty.[2] For example, an organization that does an initial investigation of payment patterns can have a good idea of when particular clients will pay. Let's assume, for example, that one customer who routinely pays his or her balance between the certain days of the month has not paid a week after his or her usual payment date. By applying Big Data analytics, an alert would be automatically generated with triggers to follow-up actions. A call to the customer might be made, or an automated email notification sent to notify the customer regarding the delayed payment. There are several advantages to this approach. If there is no exception, other than poor follow-up by the customer's accounts payable (AP) department, the notifications should prompt corrective action. This is also a more timely and preferable approach to other more punitive actions. Resolving accounts receivable (AR) issues sooner enhances cash flow, and if your organization made a mistake, the client would be upset when you demand payment.

Another use for Big Data in receivables is the identification of clients who are routinely late in paying their bills. This can result in internal company discussions about possible solutions such as restricting credit or discovering approaches to elicit quicker payments.

---

[2] Robert Kugel, "Finance Can Get a Big Advantage from Big Data," Ventana Research, November 16, 2013, robertkugel.ventanaresearch.com/ 2013/ 11/ 16/ finance-can-get-a-big-advantage-from-big-data/ , Accessed 3/ 31/ 20176

As valuable as data analysis is for estimating, it may be significantly more profitable when connected to audits and cautions. Data analysis can identify a pattern against which actual payments can be compared. This can create an early warning system when payments deviate from expected timeframes. When customers are in financial difficulty, it is normal procedure for them to ignore their vendors (in this case—your organization.)

What are some ways that an organization could support AR with Big Data that the organization may not have used in the past?

- Search streaming media (social media, google alerts, and the like) for any comments about the financial health of the customer.
- Track additional remittance information that may suggest that payments are being held by the customer.
- Determine customer's financial position as opposed to industry benchmarks.
- Evaluate historical change in credits that were taken or disputed items.

KNOWLEDGE CHECK

2. Which item was NOT listed as a way to help process and collect AR?

    a. Search streaming media.
    b. Search unstructured remittance information.
    c. Create an effective dunning process.
    d. Stratify AR and focus on the top 80 percent of value.

Accounts Payable (AP)

Given the sheer amount of data contained within AP, predictive analysis is the most value-adding process. Many have said that they are assessing data inside the vendor master document, although others said that the focus of their predictive analysis was the areas of purchasing-to-payment analysis, review of operating disbursement (with the primary attention being given to AP), and validation of payments to vendors.[3]

Duplicate Detection

One often overlooked procedure that can be applied to asset recovery is a duplicate payment check. It is a method to discover recovery dollars, accounting mistakes, outliers, fraud, or anomalies. Big Data can drastically reduce the amount of time needed to investigate duplicate payments, invoices, transactions, and vendor returns for credit.

An annual download is recommended for the disbursement data. The data should be sorted in a spreadsheet based on invoice numbers, dates, amounts, and the like. Keep in mind that traditional safeguards built into AP systems have long been overridden by AP clerks with the simple addition of a "dash" or addition of an "A" to fool the software that the invoice is original.

---

[3] Ibid.

KNOWLEDGE CHECK

3. What tool was recommended to check for duplicate payments?

    a. An outsourced financial person.

    b. A database.

    c. A spreadsheet.

    d. Streaming data.

Sampling

Sampling is a major aspect of audit work, and with such a variety of approaches to use, it is no surprise that sampling is one of the leaders in adding value to data analysis. One popular tool is using IDEAs statistical sampling techniques to set the scope. With good statistical analysis, the results can be extrapolated to the overall population of data. Statistical functions, summarizations, and stratifications help leadership analyze data to make projections and assess past performance.

Stratified sampling can be used to look at losses and gains on backdated trades, to stratify invoices and payment, and to execute random sampling. Data analytics is likewise used to test and perform unique word searches. One of the numerous advantages data analysis technology offers the capability to break down the data of an entire population, in contrast to sampling that only looks at a percentage. Regardless, data analysis permits you to join, sort, and summarize information to analyze smaller sets of data.

Data Imports, Extractions, and Analysis

For most auditors and accounting experts, the greatest difficulty is knowing where to apply data analysis—getting the needed information and importing it into an analysis tool. Data analysis programming engineers have made vast innovations to disentangle data imports, using tools like PDF converters, drag-and-drop abilities, and the extension of data capacity limits. New technology also allows for extraction within specific criteria (such as name or client codes). And tools like IDEA and ODBC can save hundreds of work hours over MS query or SQL because they allow for more efficient downloads, examinations, and summarized information.

Auditors are using data analysis to perform large downloads of financial transactions, alongside synopses and analytics, to help scope and test amid the review. For example, an internal auditor in the health services industry is using data analysis to acquire payment data from an enterprise resource planning application to review for payment dates on weekends, duplicate record search, and account coding errors.

Continuous Auditing and Monitoring

Data analysis is used to automate manual procedures and regularly test systems via continuous monitoring. Special programs can be implemented to establish nonstop review scripts to detect data entry errors as well as exceptions to travel and entertainment, budget and financial statement exceptions, procurement cards, HR, and accounts payable.

Though monitoring can identify real-time exceptions, it is usually more feasible for accountants to process only monthly or quarterly. Continuous monitoring will be a function of the likelihood of an error, the magnitude of an error, or the other controls in place.

Other areas that should be considered for continuous monitoring are regulatory compliance, credit information, market data, financial information, and any other major changes.

Also, consider monitoring major industry trends and company trends via the following:

- Google alerts
- Social media posts, tweets, and the like
- Criminal postings
- Management and discussion analysis from SEC reports

KNOWLEDGE CHECK

4. Which of these was NOT listed as a difficulty in Big Data analysis?

    a. Where to apply data analysis.
    b. Acquiring the necessary information.
    c. Having the right tool to analyze the data.
    d. Importing the data into the system.

Fraud Detection and Monitoring

Though you may discover fraud when looking for anomalies or oddities, many accountants are using data tools as a scientific device to hunt down fraud and schemes. Data analysis tools permit the review of information from diverse perspectives to identify the real cause of the fraudulent situation. Some of the ways data analysis is being used to look for patterns of fraud include trend analysis, behavioral analysis, and changes in spending patterns.

Analysis of Procurement Cards

Procurement cards have reduced the amount of administrative work required to handle the processing of small purchases and posting of transactions. However, procurement cards have resulted in additional control risks. Although procurement cards have helped "lean" accounts payable departments, they must be managed with appropriate controls to diminish abuse and waste. Accountants must examine the activity continuously to analyze trends and spending patterns. The same processes to manage accounts payable should be conducted for aggregate procurement cards and individual procurement cards. If inappropriate behavior is occurring, it should be detected in the analytics process.

Payroll and Time Sheets

Chasing down errors or fraud related to timesheets and payroll can be time-consuming for auditors. Respondents to a survey conducted by Audimation Services stated that they execute "weekly payroll dollar or total reasonableness testing," or they perform 30+ examination systems on a quarterly premise covering purchase-pay, revenue, journal entries and payroll.[4] Data analysis is also adding value by surveying electronic time and attendance records for consistency and compliance with existing arrangements, systems, and work regulations.

---

[4] "Top 10 Areas Where Data Analysis Is Adding the Most Value," SAMA, 2011, www.samaaudit.com/ software/ caseware-idea/ top-10-areas-where-data-analysis-is-adding-the-most-value.html, Accessed 3/ 31/ 17

A respondent said they had reduced "the time required to review payroll prior to [our] weekly transmission to ADP from several hours to less than 30 minutes."[5]

Joins and Comparisons

One of the greatest qualities data analysis conveys the capacity to join databases and records to sort, summarize, and investigate information. This enables the ability to look at information from distinctive points to track exceptions, misrepresentations, blunders, and other data. When databases or files are joined, they can be used to check for anomalies, perform inventory turnover analysis and stock analysis, extract data from PDFs to create a new analysis, reconcile outstanding checklists, and replace manual conversion processes.

Some examples of ways that joining processes can be used to compare sets of data are:

- Active application user accounts against a list of terminated employees
- Physician scheduling system compared to the billing system
- Vendor terms including days paid early and aged receivables
- Missing invoice numbers
- Employee and HR records compared to vendor address
- Tax ID numbers and conflict of interest
- Review of billing and pricing agreements against contract agreements

Inventory Audits

Analytic tools are also being used to analyze inventories. They can be used in the following ways:

- Inventory audits
- Identify slow moving items
- Identify obsolete items
- Reconcile the inventory counts
- Conduct test counts
- Fixed asset inventories

Centralized Accounting and Data Mining

When companies have a centralized database, it is easier to perform data mining analysis. Consider vendor analysis, customer analysis, expense analysis, journal entry analysis, and the like.

Compliance

Data analysis is valuable in meeting industry and documentation requirements. An internal audit function can use data analysis for arranging, executing, and reporting SOX compliance as well as reviews of other areas and procedures.

Data Warehousing

Data analytics is being used to help create data warehousing strategies incorporating legacy systems.

---

[5] Ibid.

Population Testing

In the past, data analysis was limited in its ability to gather large volumes of data that could be accessed, massaged, and analyzed. Data analytics today allows this ability and, as a result, the amount of data can be increased—possibly to the entire data population as opposed to relying on sample data and a corresponding extrapolation.

Reconciliation

The power of data analytics allows greater analysis and reconciliation of data. Some governmental contracts require great accuracy. However, the volume of data and the reporting levels made this requirement difficult to maintain prior to data analytics.

Revenue Reporting

Using data analysis for revenue reporting enables the combination of disparate databases, making corporate-wide reporting quicker and more efficient. Similar to the way it can enhance and improve government reporting, data analytics has also improved the ability to calculate revenue recognition at a level that was previously not feasible.

Creative Uses

Respondents to the Audimation survey also noted some other creative uses for data analytics, including the following:

- Hourly energy bidding analysis
- Analyzing client behaviors around periods of renewal
- Analyzing surveys provided by customers
- Measuring the adequacy of a promotional program
- Analyzing of student enrollment
- Reviewing billing
- Monitoring the Foreign Corrupt Practices Act
- Integrating of student data with online learning systems
- Appraising risks
- Analyzing bad medical debt
- Testing data in different system logs
- Analyzing wire exceptions in banking systems
- Evaluating loans and analyzing portfolios[6]

PREDICTIVE ANALYTICS AND ACCOUNTING

What is the role of predictive analytics and the accounting department? Review the following definition from chapter 1:

> Predictive analytics is the practice of extracting information from existing data sets to determine patterns and predict future outcomes and trends. Predictive analytics does not tell you what will

---

[6] Ibid.

happen in the future. It forecasts what might happen in the future with an acceptable level of reliability, and includes what-if scenarios and risk assessment.[7]

How Nissan Used Predictive Analytics to Survive a Natural Disaster

Predictive analytics can create a competitive advantage for your company that could even help it weather a natural disaster. Consider Nissan and the 2011 tsunami. Japan was crushed by an earthquake and the subsequent tsunami on March 11, 2011, that killed more than 20,000 people and severely damaged the Fukushima Daiichi nuclear plant.

As the country began to recover, it was clear that the effect on the worldwide economy and Japanese organizations would be massive. Harm to organizations in Japan would bring about enormous supply chain disturbances all through the world.

The data analysis of John Wilenski, CPA, CGMA, at Nissan Motor Co. Ltd played a significant part in helping Nissan remain afloat amidst the aftermath.

More than 45 of Nissan's critical suppliers suffered serious harm as a result of the catastrophe, according to research by the Massachusetts Institute of Technology (MIT) and Pricewaterhouse Coopers.[8] Fortunately for Nissan, analytics gathered before the quake of its supply chain helped the organization use sound judgment afterward in the rebuilding process. This success was part of the process created by Wilenski to monitor Nissan's vendors.

Nissan used budgetary information and data provided by supplier CFOs, often updated weekly or even daily. Wilenski's group created different models for evaluating suppliers' financial health, including a cash flow assessment tool, a stress test with "what-if" scenarios of suppliers and a break-even tool. These tools were based on supplier information and global economic data. This process allowed Nissan to determine which suppliers would survive the calamity and which suppliers would need help.

MIT and PwC report stated that solid risk management and viable countermeasures helped Nissan end 2011 with a 9.3 percent improvement in productions, contrasted with the stark 9.3 percent decrease across the entire industry.[9]

Ten Keys to Executing Data Analysis

Wilenski is building a predictive investigation tool for higher education. Here are his 10 suggestions to implement data analysis:[10]

- Distinguish the business objective.
  - Predict bankruptcy or default?
  - Minimize risk?
  - Increase profitability?
  - Lessen costs?
  - Retain employees?
  - Draw in new clients?

---

[7] "Predictive Analytics," Webopedia, www.webopedia.com/ TERM/ P/ predictive_analytics.html
[8] Ken Tysiac, "Use Predictive Analytics to Thrive— nd Survive," *CGMA Magazine*, October 20, 2014 www.cgma.org/ magazine/ features/ pages/ predictive-analytics-20149618.aspx?TestCookiesEnabled= redirect
[9] Ibid.
[10] Ibid.

- Find data sources.
  - Company-owned systems
  - Outside sources
    - Government
    - Association
    - Public database
    - Unstructured or streaming data
  - Surveys
- Build at the lowest level of detail.
- Verify that information is accurate, timely, and helpful.
- Determine the quality of data.
- Figure out which information may be predictive. It may be necessary to aggregate data and determine its correlation.
- Automate and computerize with the possibility of human interaction and intervention.
- Communicate simply and in the language of your audience.
- Be collaborative. Get support and insight.
- Continually improve the model.

ANALYTICAL PROGRAMS AT THE SEC

The following excerpt was from the speech "Has Big Data Made Us La2y," delivered by Scott W. Bauguess, Deputy Director and Deputy Chief Economist, DERA to the American Accounting Association in the Fall of 2016. Note the ways that the SEC is utilizing Big Data in his comments.

Why are these different perspectives important for how we approach data analytics at the SEC? I've been at the Commission for nearly a decade. During that time, I have worked on a large number of policy issues. The economic analyses that have supported these policy decisions are predominantly grounded in the theory-driven research of social scientists. They rely on carefully constructed analyses that seek to address causal inference, which is crucial to understanding the potential impact of a new regulation.

But in the last few years, I've witnessed the arrival of increasingly complex data and new analytical methods used to analyze them. And some of these analytical methods are allowing analyses of previously impenetrable information sets—for example, those without structure, such as freeform text. This has been of particular interest to the SEC, where registrant filings are often in the form of a narrative disclosure. So, as a result, we have begun a host of new initiatives that leverage the machine learning approach to behavioral predictions, particularly in the area of market risk assessment, which includes the identification of potential fraud and misconduct.

Today, the SEC, like many other organizations, is adopting these new methodologies at a very rapid pace. Of course, this is not to say that we are letting go of classical statistical modeling. And, as I would like to focus on now, none of our analytical programs, whether grounded in classical statistical modeling or machine learning, can replace human judgment, which remains essential in making the output of our analytical models and methods actionable. To understand why let me give you some examples.

Let me begin with the Corporate Issuer Risk Assessment Program, also known as CIRA, which relies on classical statistical modeling developed by DERA economists and accountants in collaboration with expert staff in the SEC's Division of Enforcement. This program grew out of an initiative originally referred to as the "accounting quality model," or, AQM, which was itself rooted in academic research. In particular, AQM focused on estimates of earnings quality and indications of inappropriate managerial discretion in the use of accruals. As former DERA Division Director and SEC Chief Economist Craig Lewis noted, "[a]cademics in finance and accounting have long studied the information contained in financial statements to better understand the discretionary accounting choices that are made when presenting financial information to shareholders."[iv]

Today, the CIRA program includes these modeling measures of earnings quality as part of more than two hundred thirty (230) custom metrics provided to SEC staff. These include measures of earnings smoothing, auditor activity, tax treatments, key financial ratios, and indicators of managerial actions. Importantly, they are readily accessible by SEC staff through an intuitive dashboard customized for their use. Referencing DERA's collaboration with the Division of Enforcement's FRAud Group, Enforcement Division Director Andrew Ceresney noted earlier this year, "CIRA provides us with a comprehensive overview of the financial reporting environment of Commission registrants and assists our staff in detecting anomalous patterns in financial statements that may warrant additional inquiry."[v]

However, this was not how the press first reported on the original initiative when it coined the term "Robocop" to describe it—as if a machine makes the important decisions in identifying potential market risks. As our current DERA Director and Chief Economist Mark Flannery recently noted, "this implied perspective is at best inaccurate and at worst misleading. While these activities use quantitative analytics designed to help prioritize limited agency resources, the tools we in DERA are developing do not—indeed cannot—work on their own."[vi]

But at the same time, some of the most exciting developments at the Commission have centered on machine learning and text analytics. While machine learning methods have been around since the 1950s,[vii], it is the arrival of big data and high-performance computing environments that have advanced their uses. At the Commission, this has taken on several forms. At the most basic level, and consistent with methods that are now commonplace in academic research, we have extracted words and phrases from narrative disclosures in forms and filings. For example, by applying a programming technique that uses human-written rules to define patterns in documents, referred to as "regular expressions," [viii] we are able to systematically measure and assess how emerging growth companies are availing themselves of JOBS Act provisions through what they disclose in their registration statements.

More recently, we have adopted topic modeling[ix] methods to analyze tens of thousands of narrative disclosures contained in registrant filings. For those of you not familiar with topic modeling, when applied to a corpus of documents, it can identify groups of words and phrases across all documents that pertain to distinct concepts ("topics") and simultaneously generate the distribution of topics found within each specific document. We are also performing sentiment analysis using natural language processing techniques to assess the tonality[x] of each filing—for example, identify those with a negative tone, or a tone of obfuscation. We then map these topic and tonality "signals" into known measures of risk—such as examination results or past enforcement actions—using machine learning algorithms. Once trained, the final model can be applied to new documents as they are filed by registrants, with levels of risk assigned on the basis of historical findings across all filers. This process can be applied to different types of disclosures, or to unique categories of registrants, and the results then used to help inform us on how to prioritize where investigative and examination staff should look.

While this machine-learning approach to text analytics has provided a new and exciting way to detect potential market misconduct, just as with classical modeling methods, it does not work on its own. In particular, while a model may classify a filing as high risk, the classification does not provide a clear indicator of potential wrongdoing. To the contrary, many machine learning methods do not generally point to a particular action or conduct indicative of fraud or other violation. The human element remains a necessary part of the equation.[11]

Note: the roman numeral references included in the speech are as follows:

[iv] Craig Lewis, Chief Economist and Director, Division of Risk, Strategy, and Financial Innovation, U.S. Securities & Exchange Commission, Financial Executives International Committee on Finance and Information Technology, Dec. 13, 2012.

[v] Andrew Ceresney, Director, Division of Enforcement, U.S. Securities & Exchange Commission, Directors Forum 2016 Keynote Address.

[vi] Mark Flannery, Director, Division of Economic and Risk Analysis, U.S. Securities & Exchange Commission, Global Association of Risk Professionals Risk Assessment Keynote Address.

[vii] See Arthur L. Samuel, Some Studies in Machine Learning Using the Game of Checkers, IBM Journal, Vol. 3, No. 3, July 1959.

[viii] Thompson, K. (1968). "Programming Techniques: Regular expression search algorithm." Communications of the ACM. 11 (6): 419–422. doi:10.1145/363347.363387.

[ix] See, for example, *David Blei, "Probabilistic Topic Models," Communications of the ACM. 55, April 2012.*

[x] See, e.g., Tim Loughran and Bill McDonald, 2011, "When is a Liability not a Liability? Textual Analysis, Dictionaries, and 10-Ks," Journal of Finance, 66:1, 35-65.

Exercise: How many Big Data techniques are being used by the SEC and how could they be utilized by the accounting department?

_____

_____

_____

---

[11] https://www.sec.gov/news/speech/bauguess-american-accounting-association-102116.html

Practice Questions

1. What type of data should be accessed to increase value?

2. What were some of the sources for industry trends?

3. Describe the steps to creating a predictive analytics program.

Chapter 9

ETHICS AND PRIVACY WITH BIG DATA

INTRODUCTION

One of the biggest drawbacks to Big Data is the potential for violation of individual privacy. In this chapter, we will examine examples of Big Data that have been used in ways that might be hurtful to an individual or intrusive from a privacy aspect. It is important that every organization evaluate how Big Data affects its ethics policies.

ETHICAL QUESTIONS

Throughout this text, we have considered many different examples of Big Data. Unfortunately, ethical implications of use, accumulation, or sharing of that data have not kept pace with the vast increase in the volume of Big Data. Consider the following situations:

- Data that is pushed by the owner to a provider (even with access permission) that the data owner is unaware of.
- Data that the user is aware of but has not given permission to access like personal photos.
- Data that the user is aware of but never thought that it would be used for such purposes, for example
  - insurance and health information, or
  - texting status (especially when there is an accident).
- Data that is collected from Internet surfing patterns.
- Data embedded in other objects such as video, audio, or photo.
- Ownership of Big Data generated by the individual which becomes part of a larger database.
- Are the assumptions and conclusions that you or your company make about employees or prospective employees appropriate?
- What unstructured Big Data, does your organization have that it is not using but could be used by someone else if they obtained access to it? (Think email.)

KNOWLEDGE CHECK

1. The current state of ethics policies, as they relate to Big Data, are

    a. Ethics policies are fine as they exist today.
    b. Ethics policies have not kept pace with the explosion of Big Data.
    c. Ethics policies just need minor tweaks to incorporate Big Data.
    d. Big Data policies are already addressed by IT policies.

ETHICAL IMPLICATIONS[1]

Forbes shared an article on the ethics of Big Data in March 2014. The article raised interesting implications that could be used to create a framework for Big Data policies.

Just because Big Data is prevalent, it does not mean that privacy does not exist. It is imperative that the rules for privacy are defined. Where does the data come from? Who owns the data? What rights does a gatherer must accumulate, use and maintain data? Individuals ought to be able to deal with the stream of their private data crosswise over various communication frameworks. Determine what the difference between shared data and public data is. Unfortunately, many of our modern conveniences are designed to produce private information (GPS, Wi-Fi, cell towers, and the like). However, just because we (or our

---

[1] Jonathan H. King and Neil M. Richards, "What's Up with Big Data Ethics?" *Forbes*, March 28, 2014, www.forbes.com/ sites/ oreillymedia/ 2014/ 03/ 28/ whats-up-with-big-data-ethics/ . Accessed 3/ 31/ 17

equipment) generate health, financial, location information, and so forth, it does not mean that anyone can assume ownership or use of that data.

Big Data requires full disclosure as to its access, archive, and usage. This can be especially confusing when companies have access to information that can be put to a new use and gain insights that they never had before (consider the Target pregnancy example.) For Big Data to fit within generally accepted mores, the accumulators of Big Data must be forthright of how individual information is being utilized or even sold.

Identities are vulnerable with Big Data. It is possible to determine an individual's identity without their knowledge or permission. There also is an individual responsibility to understand the impact that one's identity could have should it be revealed or theorized. For example, what would be the effect if we could identify the IPO clients of investment bankers based on Big Data? Would it not be possible to make assumptions that would be advantageous in stock transactions? But would it be ethical?

What is your organization doing to protect its data? Consider Edward Snowden and Chelsea (Bradley) Manning of Wikileaks, what resides in your corporate email?

EXAMPLES OF BIG DATA ETHICAL LAPSES

Let's briefly examine four major events in Big Data lapses:

- Target and customer information
- Google's location history
- Eric Snowden
- Julian Assange and WikiLeaks

Target and the Danger of Predictive Analytics[2]

As noted in chapter seven, Target was able to use Big Data for customer information and then use predictive analytics to predict the likelihood of pregnancy. How had Target obtained information from customers without spying on them and how do you take advantage of that information?

According to The New York Times, Target hired Andrew Pole as a statistician in 2002. Pole had a master's degree in statistics and another in economics. Staff from Target's marketing department approached Pole and asked him if he could determine whether a customer was expecting a baby. If this could be achieved, Target could market to the customer prior to the birth and hopefully garner a larger portion of "future spending" related to the baby needs.

What type of data does Target acquire on its customers? When the opportunity arises, Target assigns each shopper a unique code—known internally as the guest ID number—that keeps tabs on everything purchased.

---

[2] Charles Duhigg, "How Companies Learn Your Secrets," *The New York Times*, February 16, 2012, www.nytimes.com/ 2012/ 02/ 19/ magazine/ shopping-habits.html?pagewanted= all&_r= 0 Accessed 3/ 31/ 17

The following are linked to the Guest ID:

- Use of credit card
- Use of a coupon
- Completion of a survey
- Mailed in a refund
- Call to the customer helpline
- Opened an email
- Visited Target website

The following additional demographic information is also linked to Guest ID: age, marital status, children, address, driving time to store, your estimated salary, recent relocation history, your credit cards, and websites you visit.

In addition, Target can buy additional data such as ethnicity, job history, the magazines you read, bankruptcy history, marital (divorce) history, the year you bought (or lost) your house, your college, online topics you participate in, preferred coffee brands, type of paper towels, cereal or applesauce, your political perspectives, reading habits, charitable giving, and the vehicles that you have.

To appreciate the relationship between predictive analytics and buying habits, the writer of the *New York Times* article, Charles Duhigg, highlighted some foundational research conducted in the 1980s by a team of researchers led by UCLA professor, Alan Andreasen. The research studied purchases such as soap, toothpaste, trash bags, and toilet paper. Most shoppers paid little attention to how they bought these products. These were habitual purchases and did not involve any complex decision making.

The researchers found that when some customers were going through a major life event like graduation, a new job, moving, or the like, shopping habits became flexible and predictable. If the habits were predictable, the retailers could capitalize on this knowledge. They also discovered that newlyweds changed coffee brands. The purchase of a new house results in new breakfast cereal choices and finally, divorce results in buying different brands of beer. Therefore, shopping habits would also be expected to change for a mother expecting a child.

Target had traditional indicators of motherhood such as a baby-shower registry, which became a source of data for Pole. Pole's research identified about 25 products that, when analyzed together, enabled the ability to assign each shopper a "pregnancy prediction" score. He could also estimate the due date so Target could send coupons timed to very specific stages of her pregnancy.

Pole applied the "pregnancy prediction" score to every regular female shopper in Target's national database and created a list of tens of thousands of women who were most likely pregnant. These shoppers could now be targeted for specific marketing programs.

Supposedly, about a year after the pregnancy-prediction model was created, an irate man walked into a Minneapolis Target to see the manager. He was angry that his daughter received coupons that an expectant mother would receive and wondered whether the store was encouraging teenage pregnancy (his daughter was still in high school.)

The manager apologized and then called a few days later to apologize again. On the phone, though, the father was somewhat abashed. "I had a talk with my daughter," he said. "It turns out there has been some activities in my house I haven't been completely aware of. She's due in August. I owe you an apology."[3]

Exercise: What is the implication of companies gathering data on customers, making predictive analytics and then sending advertising material based on the marketing data?

_____

_____

_____

KNOWLEDGE CHECK

2. Target assigns a unique code to each shopper known as a

    a. Guest ID.
    b. Shopper ID.
    c. Customer ID.
    d. Target Partner ID

3. Target's research team found that approximately how many products, when taken as a group, could be a good pregnancy indicator?

    a. 25.
    b. 30.
    c. 35.
    d. 37.

GOOGLE'S LOCATION HISTORY IS RECORDING

If you have an Android device, Google could be following and recording your locations and movement.

The tracking is a result of an overlooked component in Android called Google Location History. The application itself is not surprising. It uses cell towers and Wi-Fi to find your device and you. Apple and Microsoft also use similar applications in their devices.

The thing about the Google Location administration is that, although the standard Android setup routine asks whether you want to activate it, it does not mention that you can turn it off.

Google Location History is another matter of itself.

_____

[3] Gus Lubin, "The Incredible Story of How Target Exposed a Teen Girl's Pregnancy," *Business Insider*, February 16, 2012, www.businessinsider.com/ the-incredible-story-of-how-target-exposed-a-teen-girls-pregnancy-2012-2 Accessed 3/ 31/ 17

Consider what Google says beneath the Location choices:

> "Google's location program utili2es Wi-Fi and other signals to determine your location. The program may store some of this information on your device and may gather other information from your device at the same time."

GPS is not always necessary as the device can access cell sites and Wi-Fi signals. These can result in lower battery usage and, therefore, be more desirable. However, this process indicates that the signals will be both "anonymous" and "collected." It is not anonymous, as the information is tied to your account, and the activities are being recorded.

To check if you have Location History enabled, go to the Google Maps Location History page (https://maps.google.com/locationhistory/). Use the gear-icon button to access history settings and choose disabled or enabled.

Realize that disabling location history does not remove history. It is possible to erase the past 30 days of information from the location history page. The default time shows location history for the current day, so you may not see any plots on the map.

The technology review website c| net has laid out the technique to find this information on your phone. Use the calendar to the left to show your history for up to 30 days. If you have been tracked during this timeframe, the specific points will appear on the map. Below the calendar, there are options to delete your history from the time you have chosen or to delete all history.[4] It is possible to shut off this tracking or delete portions of the history.

---

[4] Matt Elliott, "Where to Find the Map That Shows Google Is Tracking Your Location," c| *net*, November 5, 2015, www.cnet.com/how-to/how-to-delete-and-disable-your-google-location-history/ Accessed 3/31/17

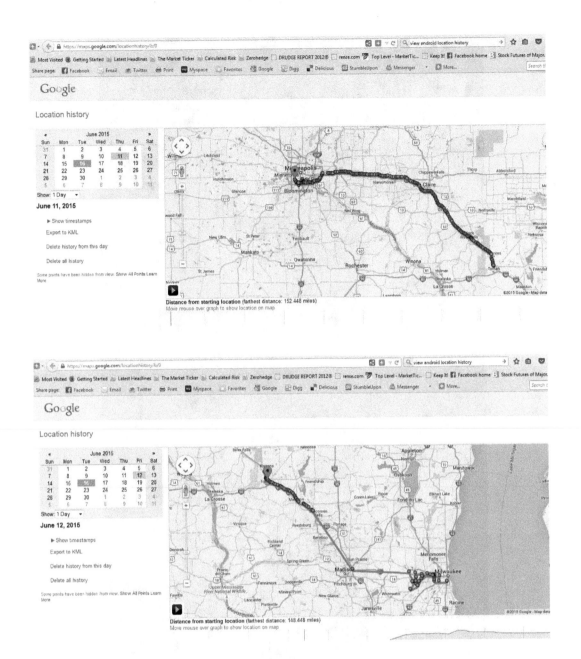

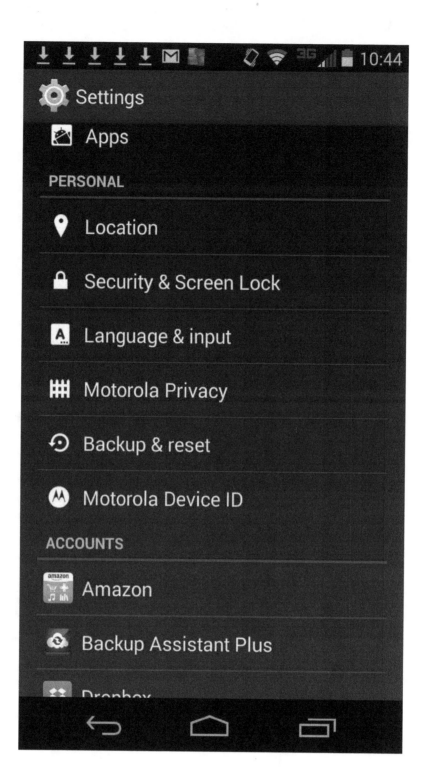

It is possible to zoom in and see all of the points that your mobile device connected to during a particular day.

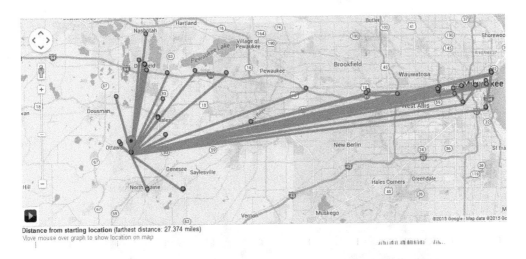

Distance from starting location (farthest distance: 27.374 miles)
Move mouse over graph to show location on map

Every dot on the map is a point where Google used Wi-Fi Positioning System (WPS) to locate this cell phone. Every time the cell phone connected to a Wi-Fi access point, the MAC address and SSID would be sent to Google's servers. This information using GPS and cell ID data is then collected and stored. This becomes the source of the Google Location History map.[5]

There are some benefits to using this service. For instance, to make airline travel easier, your boarding pass can be automatically displayed on your phone as the cell identifies your arrival at the airport.

Keeping the history can also be helpful for your daily commute so that weather and traffic information is available before you begin the drive.

Unfortunately, there is little control to customize the information retained by Google. It is an "all or nothing" type of data storage. The following items are not controllable:

- It is not possible to limit how long location data is retained.
- It doesn't expire automatically.
- History cannot be retained for one day, one week or one month (note: history for any period, from one to 30 days, can be erased).

---

[5] "Google's Location History Is Still Recording Your Every Move," *How-To Geek*, accessed March 22, 2016, www.howtogeek.com/ 195647/ googles-location-history-is-still-recording-your-every-move/ Accessed 3/ 31/ 17

With the Android device, the location services settings are easy to change. The first step is to open the location settings as shown in the following screenshot.

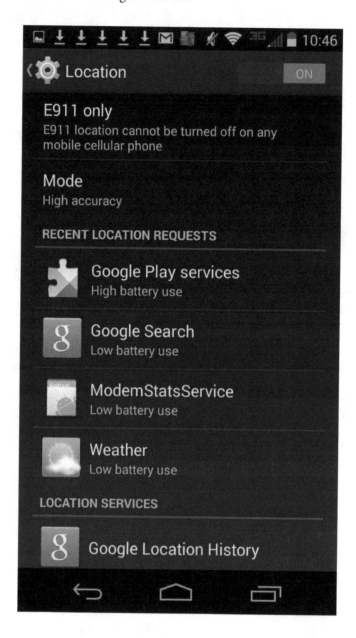

It is possible to simply turn off the location settings about anything on your device reporting your location. Turning off the location will render certain apps unusable.

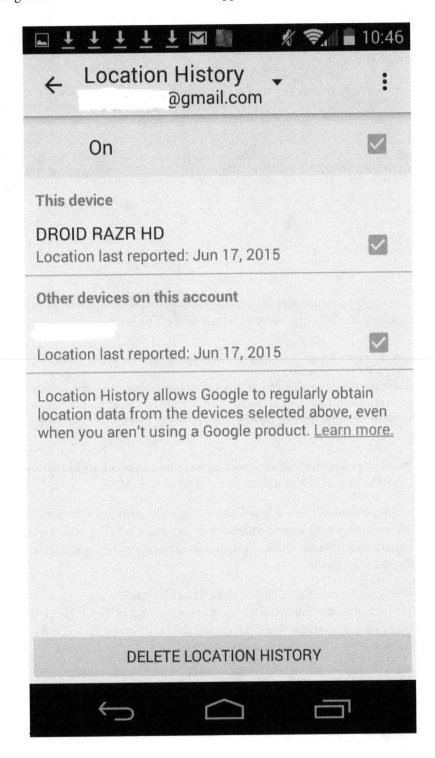

There is the option to turn off location reporting completely. Or, leave location reporting enabled and turn off location history.

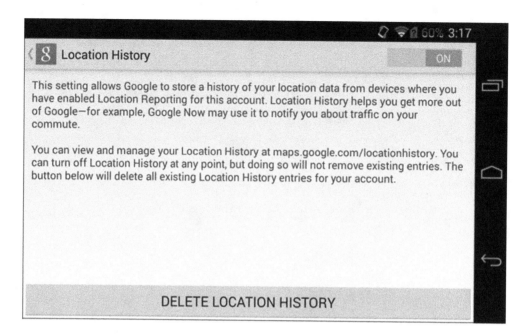

It is possible to wipe your entire location history by clicking on the "Delete Location History" button.

Apple device users can turn off Google's location reporting, but cannot wipe the history from the mobile device. It will be necessary to visit the Google Map Location History page mentioned previously. Remember that additional Android devices may also be recording history (see preceding image for other connected devices.)

The Google Location History has practical uses, such as tracking and watching family members, tracking your work mileage, or following trip progressions from location to location.

The problem is that Google does not let the user know in a simple form that they are being tracked. Thus, confidential information can be shared without realizing that it is being collected. Google should consider adding on option during setup to allow the user to understand the implications of location history and the ability to easily opt out.

An unscrupulous person with access to the mobile device can add another account, turn off the syncing process or indications from that account and then track the real owner of the device. If this is done without the knowledge of the original owner of the device, the implications could be disturbing.

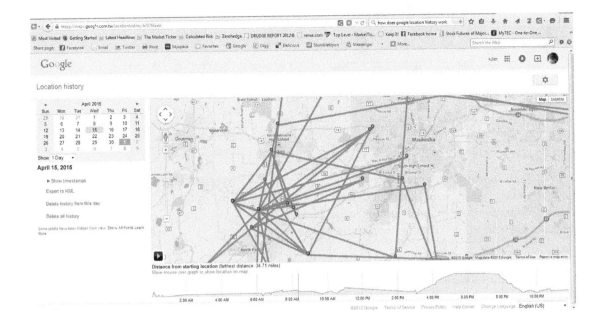

KNOWLEDGE CHECK

4. If you disable the Google Location History, what happens?

    a. All past history is removed.

    b. All past history for the last 30 days remains.

    c. All past history is unaffected.

    d. Google Location will not allow you to use the map feature.

5. Which of these was listed as a benefit of Location History being active?

    a. Obtaining your boarding pass as you arrive at the airport.

    b. Finding a lost device.

    c. Recognizing network associates that may be nearby.

    d. Determining whether sales staff are visiting customers.

6. Which was a Location History danger outlined previously?

    a. An unscrupulous person may find a way to track your movement.

    b. Your boss could ask for your phone to account for your whereabouts.

    c. Your location based on your history may become part of a legal investigation.

    d. Your location history may provide clues about mergers and acquisitions.

Exercise: How could this mapping feature be used to benefit your company? How could it be misused to hurt your business? What are the implications for our private lives?

_____

_____

_____

Loss of Privacy—Big Data Security Leaks

These last couple of years have been nothing short of astounding with the theft of confidential information from email systems and their corresponding release to the public. As a country, we have been shocked, intrigued, frightened, apprehensive and are still in a state of uncertainty as to what information will be revealed by either Eric Snowden or Julian Assange via Wikileaks.

Julian Assange and WikiLeaks

Julian Assange is the editor-in-chief of the website WikiLeaks. He has a background in computer programming and hacking. WikiLeaks distributes sensitive data, news leaks, and whistleblower information from unidentified sources. WikiLeaks achieved notoriety in 2010 when it distributed U.S. military and political reports received from Pfc. Bradley Manning, an Army intelligence analyst. Bradley Manning was able to acquire U.S. State Department Cables. In Sept. 2011, WikiLeaks posted all of the cables unreacted. This resulted in over 100,000 or more secret U.S. diplomatic cables available on the Internet.

According to "Democracy Now!," WikiLeaks recently published leaked chapters of the secret Trans - Pacific Partnership (TPP)—a global trade deal between the United States and 11 other countries. The TPP would cover 40 percent of the global economy, but details have been concealed from the public. A recently disclosed "Investment Chapter" highlights the intent of U.S. - led negotiators to create a tribunal in which corporations can sue governments if their laws interfere with a company's claimed future profits. Assange warns the plan could chill the adoption of health and environmental regulations.[6]

DNC leaks—During the 2016 Presidential Election, Wikileaks released documents from the Democratic National Committee. The documents disclosed opinions and positions that angered the Democratic Presidential Candidates that were in the primaries for the overall Democratic Nomination for President.

CIA Vault 7 (another whistleblower)—The CIA appears to have been hacked by another individual, and confidential documents are currently being leaked to the Internet.

Exercise: Obtaining information in an unethical fashion is not the central issue in this exercise. What is the implication of the details contained in companies' systems in both document and email forms? How could the data be used against a company today?

_____

_____

_____

_____

[6] Amy Goodman, "Julian Assange on the Trans-Pacific Partnership: Secretive Deal Isn't About Trade, But Corporate Control," _Democracy Now!_ Accessed March 22, 2016, www.democracynow.org/ 2015/ 5/ 27/ julian_assange_on_the_trans_pacific

KNOWLEDGE CHECK

7. Which was the most recent leaked info from Assange's group?

    a. Affordable Care Act (ACA).
    b. Chapters of the Trans-Pacific Partnership (TPP).
    c. Benghazi papers.
    d. Petraeus affair.

Snowden

Snowden is best known for his role in stealing top-secret electronic documents from the National Security Agency. At the time, Snowden worked as an intelligence contractor for Booz Allen Hamilton in Hawaii.

This is the leak that "continues to give" as journalists have released more than 7,000 top-secret documents that Snowden entrusted them with, which some believe is less than 1 percent of the entire archive.

Snowden downloaded up to 1.5 million files, according to national intelligence officials, before jetting from Hawaii to Hong Kong to meet with journalists Glenn Greenwald and Laura Poitras. After he had handed off illegally obtained documents, he flew from Hong Kong and later became stranded in Moscow. His future is still far from certain, as the journalists he trusted started revealing his secrets.[7]

Your Company

What is the impact for your organization? Your company may have plenty of secret intangible assets (think about Coke's formulation). In addition, the company has a dearth of information contained in documents and emails that disclose strategies, M&A, employment issues and this author bets racial and sexual harassment if your company has any significant size.

Consider the following questions next time your company addresses risks or threats:

1. What information does the company maintain that could prove damaging if it was released?
    a. E-mail
    b. Electronic files
    c. Security cameras
    d. Travel information
    e. Smartphone information
    f. Conversations knowingly and unknowingly taped)
    g. Intangible assets
    h. Contracts, pricing information, and so on.
    i. Customer lists
    j. Possession of electronic company information
2. What policies are in place that specifically address the preceding items?
3. What security processes are in place for the general company, individual employees, IT employees and contractors?
4. When were the IT systems checked for vulnerabilities by a trusted, outside contractor?

---

[7] www.businessinsider.com/ snowden-leaks-timeline-2016-9

KNOWLEDGE CHECK

8. Snowden purportedly released over 7,000 documents which were estimated to be what percentage of the total files that he stole?

    a. 6 percent.
    b. 8 percent.
    c. 1 percent.
    d. 12 percent.

9. According to the text, Wikileaks released approximately how many unredacted U.S. State Department documents?

    a. 100,000.
    b. 50,000.
    c. 200,000.
    d. 250,000.

Ethics Policy Considerations[8]

What type of policies should an organization add to its existing ethics and code of conduct to address the needs of Big Data? Mark van Rijmenam of Datafloq had these suggestions:

Radical Transparency

Tell your customers in real time what information is being collected. Give users the option to remove any data that can be traced back to them. If you offer a free service, make the user aware of how any information they share in exchange for "free information" will be used. As an alternative, consider charging a fee for a service or product option that does not collect any data.

Simplicity by Design

Give users a simple option to adjust privacy settings, as well as options to determine what types of information they want to share.

Preparation and Security are Key

Determine what information is necessary for the business. Understand that data is valuable and that criminals may be interested in stealing it. Create a crisis strategy with a contingency plan in case the company gets hacked. Remind your staff of Manning and Snowden and the damage caused.

Make Privacy Part of the DNA

Consider hiring a Chief Privacy Officer (CPO) or a Chief Data Officer (CDO) who is responsible for data privacy and ethics. This individual will be accountable for data that are collected, archived, shared, or sold. Discuss the privacy and ethical issues of Big Data at the top levels of the organization.

---

[8] Mark Van Rijmenam, "Big Data Ethics: 4 Guidelines to Follow By Organizations," *Datafloq*, Accessed 3/ 31/ 17, datafloq.com/ read/ big-data-ethics-4-principles-follow-organisations/ 221

Practice Questions

1. Provide some examples of areas that would be discussed under the topic of "Rules for Privacy."

2. What were the ethical implications of Target's pregnancy prediction score?

3. How could someone secretly track your movements (or an employee, or family member, and the like)?

4. What were the four policy considerations for Big Data ethics at the end of the chapter?

INDEX

ANALYTICS AND BIG DATA
FOR ACCOUNTANTS

BY JIM LINDELL, MBA, CPA, CGMA

Solutions

DAAN GS-0417-0A

Course Code: 746272

The AICPA offers a free, daily, e-mailed newsletter covering the day's top business and financial articles as well as video content, research and analysis concerning CPAs and those who work with the accounting profession. Visit the CPA Letter Daily news box on the www.aicpa.org home page to sign up. You can opt out at any time, and only the AICPA can use your e-mail address or personal information.

Have a technical accounting or auditing question? So did 23,000 other professionals who contacted the AICPA's accounting and auditing Technical Hotline last year. The objectives of the hotline are to enhance members' knowledge and application of professional judgment by providing free, prompt, high-quality technical assistance by phone concerning issues related to: accounting principles and financial reporting; auditing, attestation, compilation and review standards. The team extends this technical assistance to representatives of governmental units. The hotline can be reached at 1-877-242-7212.

SOLUTIONS

CHAPTER 1

Practice Question Solutions

1.

Big data includes high-volume, high-velocity, and high-variety information assets that demand cost-effective, innovative forms of information processing for enhanced insight and decision making. Big Data can be classified into areas such as structured data, unstructured data, and streaming data.

2.

Descriptive, diagnostic, predictive, and prescriptive.

3.

Hadoop is a free, Java-based programming framework that supports the processing of large data sets in a distributed computing environment. It is part of the Apache project sponsored by the Apache Software Foundation.

4.

A data scientist is an employee or business intelligence consultant who excels at analyzing data, particularly large amounts of data, to help a business gain a competitive edge.

Solutions to Knowledge Check Questions

1.
   a. Incorrect. Big Data is applicable to any organization—not just multi-national companies.
   b. Correct. Structured, unstructured, and streaming data.
   c. Incorrect. Big Data goes beyond ERP systems. It includes all data: structured data, unstructured data, and streaming data.
   d. Incorrect. Big Data refers to a type of data. Serial processing is not associated with Big Data but massively parallel processing is.

2.
   a. Incorrect.1 million. Snapchat users watch nearly 7 million videos every minute.
   b. Incorrect. 4 million. Snapchat users watch nearly 7 million videos every minute.
   c. Correct. 7 million Snapchat users watch nearly 7 million videos every minute.
   d. Incorrect. 10 million. Snapchat users watch nearly 7 million videos every minute.

3.

    a.   Incorrect. A petabyte holds 5x100 billion pages. A petabyte is a 1 followed by 15 zeroes, which would approximate 500 billion pages of standard text.

    b.   Correct. A petabyte is a 1 followed by 15 zeroes, which would approximate 500 billion pages of standard text.

    c.   Incorrect. A petabyte is a 1 followed by 15 zeroes and could hold 500 billion pages of standard printer text, as opposed to 900 billion.

    d.   Incorrect. A petabyte is a 1 followed by 15 zeroes and could hold 500 billion pages of standard printer text, as opposed to 750 billion.

4.

    a.   Correct. Big Data decision making is smarter, faster, and more accurate.

    b.   Incorrect. Big Data decision making is not slower. It is faster, smarter, and more accurate.

    c.   Incorrect. Big Data decision making is not slower or more transparent. It is faster, smarter, and more accurate.

    d.   Incorrect. Big Data is smarter, faster and more accurate, as opposed to the same speed and more structured.

CHAPTER 2

Practice Question Solutions

1.

The comments should include the progression below. When the history of Big Data is viewed through the lens of accounting, it can be categorized by the interaction of the following seven different areas:

1. Bookkeeping
2. Accounting
3. Calculating machines
4. Computers
5. Internet
6. Cloud computing
7. Internet of things

2.

There are many sources of big data. The discussion could include any of the following:

1. Facebook
   a. Posts
   b. Messages
   c. Photos
   d. Consumer trends
2. Google searches
3. LinkedIn
   a. Posts
   b. Job searches
   c. Reference checking
   d. Group posts

4. Email databases
5. Retail CRM
6. Health
   a. Insurance
   b. Hospital
   c. Mental health
   d. Prisons
7. Forums
8. Social media
9. Twitter
10. RFID tags
11. Camera phones
12. GPS-enabled devices
13. Smart meters
14. Television preferences
15. YouTube
16. Music tools
17. Government databases
18. Amazon.com
    a. Other readers have selected
    b. Community chest

3.

Volume, variety, velocity, veracity

4.

There are multiple correct answers to this discussion, but could include machine sensors, customer comments in social media, customer surveys, foot traffic, cars in parking lot, pattern of returns, government or industry databases, and the like.

Solutions to Knowledge Check Questions

1.
   a. Incorrect. Lotus was not the first spreadsheet. VisiCalc was created in 1978.
   b. Incorrect. Excel was not the first spreadsheet. VisiCalc was created in 1978.
   c. Correct. VisiCalc was created in 1978.
   d. Incorrect. Multi-mate was not the first spreadsheet. VisiCalc was created in 1978.

2.
   a. Incorrect. The Roman tax code was preceded by the Code of Hammurabi.
   b. Correct. Code of Hammurabi was the earliest recording of transactions.
   c. Incorrect. The Greek merchant records were preceded by the Code of Hammurabi.
   d. Incorrect. Chinese trade records are not mentioned in the chapter, but the Code of Hammurabi is.

3.

    a.   Incorrect. The U.S. Department of Defense created the first building block for the Internet, not UCLA.

    b.   Correct. The U.S. Department of Defense created ARPANET, a computer network designed to withstand any disaster. It became the first building block for what the Internet has become today.

    c.   Incorrect. The U.S. Department of Defense created the first building block for the Internet, not Stanford.

    d.   Incorrect. The U.S. Department of Defense created the first building block for the Internet, not Harvard.

4.

    a.   Incorrect. The estimate was 420 million devices, not 240 million.

    b.   Incorrect. The estimate was 420 million devices, not 360 million.

    c.   Correct. The estimate was 420 million devices.

    d.   Incorrect. The estimate was 420 million devices, not 500 million.

CHAPTER 3

Practice Question Solutions

1.

Big Data will be used to create more customized applications for end users. Application developers will use data and analytics to create personalized, engaging experiences. The applications will try to unite related data across industries such as sports, energy, social well-being, and music. As an example, users will be able to select music based on personal preferences, such as instruments and tempo.

2.

Expert outside help needed. It is difficult to find skilled in-house talent. As a result, firms are turning to outside consultants to help with Big Data.

Solutions to Knowledge Check Questions

1.

    a.   Incorrect. Gartner expects 8.4 billion, not 4.4 billion.

    b.   Incorrect. Gartner expects 8.4 billion, not 6.8 billion.

    c.   Correct. Gartner expects 8.4 billion.

    d.   Incorrect. Gartner expects 8.4 billion, not 9.6 billion.

2.

    a.   Incorrect. According to Accenture, organizations that have completed Big Data projects are not ambivalent but satisfied with the results.

    b.   Incorrect. According to Accenture, organizations that have completed Big Data projects are not dissatisfied but satisfied with the results.

    c.   Correct. According to Accenture, organizations that have completed Big Data projects are satisfied with the results.

    d.   Incorrect. Users were satisfied, not ecstatic.

3.

    a.   Incorrect. Advanced analytics is not the most agreed-upon characteristic. File sizes > 20 TB is most agreed-upon characteristic of Big Data.

    b.   Correct. File sizes > 20TB are agreed to be characteristic of Big Data.

    c.   Incorrect. Although data from social networks is a source of Big Data, the most agreed-upon source are file sizes > 20TB.

    d.   Incorrect. File sizes > 20TB were characteristic of Big Data.

4.

    a.   Incorrect. According to the survey, 51 percent strongly agree that Big Data will revolutionize their business in the same manner that the Internet affected the business.

    b.   Incorrect. According to the survey, 39 percent strongly agree that Big Data will revolutionize their business.

    c.   Correct. Only 37 percent strongly agree that companies will lose competitive position if they do not embrace Big Data.

    d.   Incorrect. 62 percent was not mentioned. Only 37 percent strongly agree that companies will lose competitive position if they do not embrace Big Data.

5.

    a.   Incorrect. Approximately 50 percent of organizations have achieved cost as opposed to 10 percent.

    b.   Incorrect. Approximately 50 percent of organizations have achieved cost efficiencies as opposed to 30 percent.

    c.   Correct. Approximately 50 percent of organizations have achieved cost efficiencies.

    d.   Incorrect. Approximately 50 percent of organizations have achieved cost efficiencies as opposed to 70 percent.

CHAPTER 4

Practice Question Solutions

1.

To increase enterprise value for the stakeholders.

2.

- Any of the following comments could be included for change management challenges:
  - Institutional change management
  - Ensuring inter-jurisdictional collaboration and common standards
  - Different department systems that inhibit collection and organization of Big Data
  - Acquiring technically competent staff
  - Steep technical learning curve
  - Hiring qualified people
  - Barriers between departments that are cultural in nature
  - Data that are not accepted or believed
  - Data ownership, especially as it ties to organization culture
  - Lack of business sponsorship
  - Lack of belief in a business case

3.

Many tweets came from Manhattan and not from the most ravaged areas where power outages were occurring.

Solutions to Knowledge Check Questions

1.

   a. Correct. Increasing value for shareholders or stakeholders is the root objective for all activity.
   b. Incorrect. Increasing scalable architecture is a tactic for increasing value. The root objective is increasing value for stakeholders.
   c. Incorrect. Increasing Big Data capacity is a tactic for increasing value. The root objective is increasing value for stakeholders.
   d. Incorrect. Although data integration is needed, increasing value for shareholders or stakeholders is the primary objective.

2.

   a. Incorrect. Monitoring product quality is an insight achievable through Big Data. Multiple generation products are much more difficult.
   b. Incorrect. Identifying customer needs is an insight achievable through Big Data. Multiple generation products are much more difficult.
   c. Correct. Creating third- and fourth-generation products.
   d. Incorrect. Soliciting input was not mentioned, but third- and fourth-generation products was mentioned.

3.

   a. Incorrect. The top issue is data integration complexity, not lack of business sponsorship.
   b. Incorrect. The top issue is data integration complexity, not lack of skills for IT staff.
   c. Correct. Data integration complexity is the top issue.
   d. Incorrect. Data integration is the top issue, as opposed to poor data quality.

4.

   a. Correct. Using an iterative implementation strategy.
   b. Incorrect. Focusing on technology instead of the business need is a Big Data mistake.
   c. Incorrect. Not executing a cost-benefit analysis is a Big Data mistake.
   d. Incorrect. Executing multiple initiatives in parallel as part of a "big bang" approach or pilot implementations is a Big Data mistake.

CHAPTER 5

Practice Question Solutions

1.

Query and reporting, data mining, optimization, and predictive analysis are among many Big Data capabilities.

2.

Apache Hadoop is a framework that allows for storing large data sets which are distributed across clusters of computers using simple programming models and written in Java to run on a single computer on large clusters of commodity hardware computers.

3.

Map Reduce is a software model that allows large sets of data to be processed in parallel.

4.

R is a language and environment for statistical computing and graphics. It is a GNU project which is similar to the S language and environment which was developed at Bell Laboratories.

Solutions to Knowledge Check Questions

1.

   a.   Incorrect. Exploratory data analysis is finding new characteristics in data, as opposed to using statistical models for forecasting purposes.
   b.   Incorrect. Affirming existing beliefs is not exploratory data analysis, which involves finding new characteristics in data.
   c.   Correct. Finding new characteristics in data.
   d.   Incorrect. Prescribing actions is the last process; first, it is necessary to find new characteristics in data.

2.

   a.   Incorrect. Government data was listed as semi-structured.
   b.   Incorrect. Government or industry usually has semi-structured information.
   c.   Correct. Government or industry data was listed as semi-structured.
   d.   Incorrect. It was not listed as non-relational but as semi-structured.

3.

   a.   Correct. SAP did not have the infrastructure component.
   b.   Incorrect. Oracle did have infrastructure, whereas SAP did not.
   c.   Incorrect. IBM did have infrastructure, whereas SAP did not.
   d.   Incorrect. HP had an infrastructure, whereas SAP did not.

4.

   a.   Incorrect. MapR represents a complete distribution for Apache Hadoop, as opposed to a program to reduce the size of Big Data analyzed.
   b.   Incorrect. MapR is a complete, as opposed to an incomplete, distribution of Apache Hadoop.
   c.   Correct. Complete distribution for Apache Hadoop that packages more than a dozen projects.
   d.   Incorrect. It is not a relational database but a complete distribution of a dozen projects.

5.

    a. Incorrect. Teradata is a graph processing engine and not an agriculture application of Big Data.

    b. Incorrect. Teradata is a graph processing engine and not data analytics software.

    c. Correct. A native graph processing engine for graph analysis.

    d. Incorrect. It is not a relational database but a tool for graph analysis.

6.

    a. Incorrect. WolframAlpha is a specialized search engine, as opposed to data analytics software.

    b. Correct. WolframAlpha has been referred to as the "nerdy Google."

    c. Incorrect. WolframAlpha is a specialized search engine and not predictive analytics software.

    d. Incorrect. It is not a program within the MapR framework but a "nerdy Google."

7.

    a. Correct. Google Maps was illustrated using the author's consulting engagements.

    b. Incorrect. Crime statistics were illustrated with fusion tables; Google Maps was illustrated with consulting engagements.

    c. Incorrect. Google Maps was illustrated using the author's consulting engagements, not with vendor dispersion.

    d. Incorrect. Google Maps did not use post offices but crime statistics.

8.

    a. Incorrect. Hadoop is not proprietary. It's open source.

    b. Correct. Hadoop is open source.

    c. Incorrect. Hadoop is available for everyone via open source.

    d. Incorrect. Hadoop is not proprietary but open source.

9.

    a. Incorrect. Hive is a data warehousing tool, not a data cleansing program.

    b. Incorrect. Hive is a data warehousing tool, not a data analytics tool.

    c. Correct. Hive is a data warehousing and a query language.

    d. Incorrect. Hive was not designed for distributed processes but for data warehousing.

CHAPTER 6

Practice Question Solutions

1.

The discussion could include many of the items listed at the beginning of the chapter, including the following:

- Commodity versus non-commodity status
- Availability of product
- Substitute products available
- Volumes purchased
- Seasonality
- Related products purchased

2.

The Big Data from Best Buy represented the top 10 items that were searched during any given day, along with a series of data applicable to each item.

3.

For each company, there can be many different sources. The text refers to industrial production statistics and retail trade statistics as examples.

4.

Text analytics is the process of deriving high-quality information from text.

Solutions to Knowledge Check Questions

1.
   a. Incorrect. Query Builder writes queries for Best Buy data. It does not allow the creation of "what if" analysis.
   b. Incorrect. Query Builder writes queries, as opposed to disposing of electronic items no longer needed.
   c. Correct. Query Builder is an application to write custom queries for Best Buy products.
   d. Incorrect. Query Builder is not a "If this, then that" tool. It is a tool to write custom queries for Best Buy products.

2.
   a. Incorrect. Sales price was included, but discount was not.
   b. Incorrect. Regular price was included, but discount was not.
   c. Correct. The amount of discount was not included.
   d. Incorrect. Percent savings was available. The amount of discount was not included.

3.
   a. Incorrect. Best Buy query needs an API key. It does not require access to data mining software.
   b. Correct. To run the Best Buy query, it is necessary to obtain an API Key.
   c. Incorrect. Best Buy query needs an API key. It is not necessary to be able to read HTML.
   d. Incorrect. Best Buy query needs an API key.

4.
   a. Incorrect. Analytics can only ensure that the best-informed decision is made, not that the best decision is made.
   b. Incorrect. Analytics will result in a better-informed decision and may or may not result in the highest possible price to be charged.
   c. Correct. If properly used, analytics guarantees a better-informed decision.
   d. Incorrect. Analytics does not guarantee all options will be evaluated, only that a better-informed decision will be made.

5.

    a.   Incorrect. The Net Promoter Score was created by Reichheld, not Lencione.
    b.   Correct. Reichheld created the Net Promoter Score.
    c.   Incorrect. Collins wrote "Good to Great." Reichheld created the Net Promoter Score.
    d.   Incorrect. Champy was an author, not the creator of the Net Promoter Score. The creator was Reichheld.

6.

    a.   Incorrect. The Federal Reserve generates the Industrial Production Statistics, not the U.S. Census.
    b.   Incorrect. The Federal Reserve generates the Industrial Production Statistics, not the Bureau of Labor and Statistics.
    c.   Correct. The Industrial Production Statistics are generated by the Federal Reserve.
    d.   Incorrect. The Industrial Production Statistics come from the Federal Reserve, not the Small Business Administration.

7.

    a.   Correct. The NAICS for newspapers was 51111.
    b.   Incorrect. The 50001 NACIS represented the entire index. The newspaper industry was 51111.
    c.   Incorrect. The correct NAICS code for newspapers is 51111, not 54111.
    d.   Incorrect. The correct NAICS code was 50001.

8.

    a.   Correct. The monthly retail statistics are supplied by the U.S. Census.
    b.   Incorrect. The Bureau of Labor and Statistics supplies employment information; the U.S. Census supplies monthly retail statistics.
    c.   Incorrect. The Federal Reserve supplies industrial production statistics; the U.S. Census supplies monthly retail statistics.
    d.   Incorrect. The monthly retail sales statistics are obtained from the U.S. Census, not the Small Business Administration.

CHAPTER 7

Practice Question Solutions

1.

At the Consumer Electronics Show in Las Vegas, manufacturers displayed chips to improve your posture, and sports equipment (including basketballs, golf clubs, and tennis balls) to help you train smarter.

2.

Up to 25 gigabytes of data every hour

3.

MagicBand is a $1 billion investment in a wearable, sensor-loaded wristband that vacationers use to do everything from register with their inn room, purchase their lunch, experience the gates at the event congregations, and reserve a spot for particular attractions.

4.

Using IBM's predictive traffic-management software, Lyon combined real-time traffic data with advanced analytics to help the transportation department proactively manage traffic congestion.

Solutions to Knowledge Check Questions

1.
   a. Incorrect. A sensor to advise an owner when a pet wants to come in was not mentioned, but a sensor to find your lost keys was mentioned.
   b. Incorrect. A sensor for your keys was mentioned, as opposed to a sensor to notify that mail has arrived in a mailbox.
   c. Correct. A sensor to find your keys.
   d. Incorrect. No sensor was mentioned to identify someone at your front door, but a sensor was listed to find your keys.

2.
   a. Correct. One percent to 3 percent of flights canceled every day.
   b. Incorrect. The correct percent of flights canceled per day are 1 percent to 3 percent, as opposed to 2 percent to 4 percent.
   c. Incorrect. Three percent to 5 percent is not the correct percent of flights canceled every day. The actual percentage is 1 percent to 3 percent.
   d. Incorrect. Four percent to 6 percent is not the correct percent of flights canceled every day. The actual percentage is 1 percent to 3 percent.

3.
   a. Incorrect. EMI obtains music trends from many social media networks in addition to YouTube.
   b. Incorrect. EMI obtains trends from social media networks, as opposed to Google.
   c. Correct. EMI obtains music trends from social media networks.
   d. Incorrect. EMI obtains trends from social media networks; however, Instagram is known for pictures, as opposed to music.

4.
   a. Incorrect. Target has not created a marriage predictor, but a pregnancy predictor.
   b. Correct. Target has demonstrated the ability to create a pregnancy predictor for its customers.
   c. Incorrect. Target has not created an illness predictor, but a pregnancy predictor.
   d. Incorrect. Target does not say it can predict divorce, but it can predict pregnancy.

5.
   a. Correct. TempuTech can monitor grain elevators and inventory.
   b. Incorrect. TempuTech works with grain elevators, as opposed to combines.
   c. Incorrect. TempuTech works with grain elevators, as opposed to John Deere tractors.
   d. Incorrect. TempuTech was not used in fertilizer spreaders but grain elevators.

6.

    a.   Incorrect. Chase integrates its data with U.S. government data, not industry data.

    b.   Correct. Chase integrates its data with economic stats from the U.S. government.

    c.   Incorrect. Chase uses U.S. government data, as opposed to economic stats from associations.

    d.   Incorrect. Chase integrated data with economic stats from the U.S. government, not drivers' license records.

7.

    a.   Incorrect. Gnip is designed for social media streams, not for internal email systems.

    b.   Incorrect. Gnip is designed to access social media streams, not just video streams.

    c.   Correct. Gnip is designed to access social media streams.

    d.   Incorrect. Gnip is designed for social media streams, not governmental databases.

8.

    a.   Correct. Barcelona offers up-to-speed information about where to stop.

    b.   Incorrect. Barcelona offers where to stop information, not car rental information.

    c.   Incorrect. Barcelona offers up-to-date information about where to stop, not dining locations and hours.

    d.   Incorrect. It does not offer hotel accommodations but information about where to stop.

9.

    a.   Incorrect. MetLife uses Big Data to cross-sell products, not for risk analysis.

    b.   Correct. MetLife uses Big Data to cross-sell products.

    c.   Incorrect. MetLife uses Big Data to cross-sell products, not for risk evaluation with customer data.

    d.   Incorrect. MetLife uses Big Data to cross-sell products, not to identify fraudulent transactions.

CHAPTER 8

Practice Question Solutions

1.

The interesting point to keep in mind is that the data that are not being accessed in structured, unstructured, and streaming arenas have the potential to add significantly to the value created in the accounting department.

2.

Also, consider monitoring major industry trends and company trends via the following:

- Google alerts
- Social media posts, tweets, and the like
- Criminal postings
- MD&A from SEC reports

3.

1. Distinguish the business objective.
2. Find data sources.
3. Build at the lowest level of detail.
4. Verify that information is accurate, timely, and helpful.
5. Determine quality of data.
6. Figure out which information may be predictive. It may be necessary to aggregate data and determine its correlation.
7. Automate and computerize with the possibility of human interaction or intervention.
8. Communicate simply and in the language of your audience.
9. Be collaborative. Get support and insight.
10. Continually improve the model.

Solutions to Knowledge Check Questions

1.

a. Incorrect. Big Data is more important than any other innovation in recent years.
b. Incorrect. Big Data is the most important recent innovation. Lean management techniques are tactics to help make the company more efficient and profitable.
c. Correct. Big Data is applicable to enterprise financial strategies more than any other innovation seen by the CFO in recent years.
d. Incorrect. Big data is not a vehicle for seeking out wasteful practices but for enterprise financial strategies.

2.

a. Incorrect. Searching streaming media was mentioned as a tool to help reduce AR.
b. Incorrect. Searching unstructured remittance information was also mentioned as a tool to reduce AR.
c. Correct. Creating an effective dunning process is a recommended process, just not a Big Data process.
d. Incorrect. Stratification was mentioned, whereas dunning processes was not.

3.

a. Incorrect. Duplicate payment analysis can always be outsourced to a financial person. However, it will be much easier to use a spreadsheet analysis process.
b. Incorrect. A database could be configured for the analysis, but a spreadsheet would be easiest for detecting duplicate payments.
c. Correct. A spreadsheet with downloaded information is one of the best ways to check for duplicate payments.
d. Incorrect. Streaming data was not mentioned but spreadsheet analysis was.

4.

a. Incorrect. The uncertainty of where to apply data analysis is a difficulty. The right tool is not nearly as important as having the ability to import the data.
b. Incorrect. Acquiring the necessary information is a difficulty. The right tool is not nearly as important as having the ability to import the data.
c. Correct. Having the right tool is not as difficult as the ability to import the data into a tool.
d. Incorrect. Importing data was listed as a difficulty, having the right tool to analyze the data was not listed as a difficulty.

CHAPTER 9

Practice Question Solutions

1.

Where does the data come from? Who owns the data? What rights does a gatherer have to accumulate, use, and maintain data?

2.

Even if Target's prediction was accurate, what right did the company have to share information about specific products that may lead other uninformed individuals to the same pregnancy insight?

3.

An unscrupulous person with access to the mobile device can add another account; turn off the syncing process or indications from that account; and then track the real owner of the device. If this is done without the knowledge of the original owner of the device, it is very scary and potentially dangerous.

4.

Radical Transparency, Simplicity by Design, Preparation and Security are Key, Make Privacy Part of the DNA

Solutions to Knowledge Check Questions

1.
   a. Incorrect. Ethics policies are not fine as they exist today and have not kept pace with the growth in Big Data.
   b. Correct. Ethics policies have not kept pace with the explosion of Big Data.
   c. Incorrect. Ethics policies need to be reviewed and adjusted to keep pace with the growth of Big Data.
   d. Incorrect. Big Data is not addressed by IT policies and ethics policies have not kept pace with the growth of Big Data.

2.
   a. Correct. Guest ID.
   b. Incorrect. Target assigns a Guest ID, not a Shopper ID.
   c. Correct. Target assigns a Guest ID, not a Customer ID.
   d. Incorrect. The correct answer is Guest ID.

3.
   a. Correct. Target uses 25 products for the pregnancy prediction score.
   b. Incorrect. Target uses 25 products for the pregnancy prediction score, as opposed to 30.
   c. Incorrect. Target uses 25 products for the pregnancy prediction score, as opposed to 35.
   d. Incorrect. Target uses 25 products for the pregnancy prediction score, as opposed to 37.

4.
   a. Incorrect. Disabling Location History will not remove all past history.
   b. Incorrect. Disabling Location History will not affect past history.
   c. Correct. All past history is unaffected.
   d. Incorrect. The Google Maps function is still available and past history is unaffected.

5.
   a. Correct. Obtaining your boarding pass as you arrive at the airport.
   b. Incorrect. Finding a lost device could be beneficial. However, from the text, obtaining a boarding pass was highlighted.
   c. Incorrect. Recognizing network associates who may be nearby could be helpful, but obtaining your boarding pass was the example highlighted in the text.
   d. Incorrect. Tracking sales staff was not mentioned but obtaining a boarding pass was described.

6.
   a. Correct. An unscrupulous person may find a way to track your movement.
   b. Incorrect. It is possible that your boss could ask for your phone to account for your whereabouts. The text was concerned that someone may track you without your knowledge.
   c. Incorrect. There is a possibility that your location based on your history may become part of a legal investigation. The text was concerned that someone may track you without your knowledge.
   d. Incorrect. The text did not mention the potential for M&A insights but it did mention that an unscrupulous person may find a way to track your movement.

7.
   a. Incorrect. The most recent disclosure was about the TPP, not the ACA.
   b. Correct. TPP was the most recent disclosure.
   c. Incorrect. The most recent disclosure was about the TPP, not the Benghazi papers.
   d. Incorrect. The most recent leak was the TPP agreement, not the Petraeus affair.

8.
   a. Incorrect. 1 percent of the documents are estimated to have been released, not 6 percent.
   b. Incorrect. 1 percent of the documents are estimated to have been released, not 8 percent.
   c. Correct. 1 percent of the documents are estimated to have been released.
   d. Incorrect. 1 percent of the documents are estimated to have been released, not 12 percent.

9.
   a. Correct. Wikileaks released over 100,000 unredacted documents.
   b. Incorrect. Wikileaks released over 100,000 unredacted documents, not 50,000.
   c. Incorrect. Wikileaks released over 100,000 unredacted documents, not 200,000.
   d. Incorrect. Wikileaks released over 100,000 unredacted documents, not 250,000.

Users of this course material are encouraged to visit the
AICPA website at www.aicpa.org/CPESupplements
to access supplemental learning material reflecting recent
developments that may be applicable to this course.
The AICPA anticipates that supplemental materials will be
made available on a quarterly basis.

Learn More

AICPA CPE

Thank you for selecting AICPA as your continuing professional education provider. We have a diverse offering of CPE courses to help you expand your skillset and develop your competencies. Choose from hundreds of different titles spanning the major subject matter areas relevant to CPAs and CGMAs, including:

- Governmental & Not-for-Profit accounting, auditing, and updates
- Internal control and fraud
- Audits of Employee Benefit Plans and 401(k) plans
- Individual and corporate tax updates
- A vast array of courses in other areas of accounting & auditing, controllership, management, consulting, taxation, and more!

Get your CPE when and where you want

- Self-study training options that includes on-demand, webcasts, and text formats with superior quality and a broad portfolio of topics, including bundled products like –
  - CPExpress for immediate access to hundreds of one and two-credit hour online courses for just-in-time learning at a price that is right
  - Annual Webcast Pass offering live Q&A with experts and unlimited access to the scheduled lineup, all at an incredible discount.
- Staff training programs for audit, tax and preparation, compilation and review
- Certificate programs offering comprehensive curriculums developed by practicing experts to build fundamental core competencies in specialized topics
- National conferences presented by recognized experts
- Affordable AICPA courses on-site at your organization – visit **aicpalearning.org/on-site** for more information.
- Seminars sponsored by your state society and led by top instructors. For a complete list, visit **aicpalearning.org/publicseminar**.

Take control of your career development

The AICPA | CIMA Competency and Learning website at **https://competency.aicpa.org** brings together a variety of learning resources and a self-assessment tool, enabling tracking and reporting of progress toward learning goals.

Visit the AICPA store at **cpa2biz.com/CPE** to browse our CPE selections.

Just-in-time learning at your fingertips 24/7

Where can you get <u>unlimited online access</u> to 900+ credit hours (650+ CPE courses) for one low annual subscription fee?

CPExpress, the AICPA's comprehensive bundle of online continuing professional education courses for CPAs, offers you immediate access to hundreds of one and two-credit hour courses. You can choose from a full spectrum of subject areas and knowledge levels to select the specific topic you need when you need it for just-in-time learning.

Access hundreds of courses for one low annual subscription price!

How can CPExpress help you?

- ✓ Start and finish most CPE courses in as little as 1 to 2 hours with 24/7 access so you can fit CPE into a busy schedule
- ✓ Quickly brush up or get a brief overview on hundreds of topics when you need it
- ✓ Create and customize your personal online course catalog for quick access with hot topics at your fingertips
- ✓ Print CPE certificates on demand to document your training – never miss a CPE reporting deadline!
- ✓ Receive free Quarterly updates – Tax, Accounting & Auditing, SEC, Governmental and Not-For-Profit

Quantity Purchases for Firm or Corporate Accounts

If you have 10 or more employees who require training, the Firm Access option allows you to purchase multiple seats. Plus, you can designate an administrator who will be able to monitor the training progress of each staff member. To learn more about firm access and group pricing, visit aicpalearning.org/cpexpress or call 800.634.6780.

To subscribe, visit **cpa2biz.com/cpexpress**

Why AICPA?

Think of All the Great Reasons to Join the AICPA.

CAREER ADVOCACY SUPPORT
On behalf of the profession and public interest on the federal, state and local level.

PROFESSIONAL & PERSONAL DISCOUNTS
Save on travel, technology, office supplies, shipping and more.

ELEVATE YOUR CAREER
Five specialized credentials and designations (ABV®, CFF®, CITP®, PFS™ and CGMA®) enhance your value to clients and employers.

HELPING THE BEST AND THE BRIGHTEST
AICPA scholarships provide more than $350,000[1] to top accounting students.

GROW YOUR KNOWLEDGE
Discounted CPE on webcasts, self-study or on-demand courses & more than 60 specialized conferences & workshops.

PROFESSIONAL GUIDANCE YOU CAN COUNT ON
Technical hotlines & practice resources, including Ethics Hotline, Business & Industry Resource Center and the Financial Reporting Resource Center.

KEEPING YOU UP TO DATE
With news and publications from respected sources such as the *Journal of Accountancy*.

MAKING MEMBERS HAPPY
We maintain a 94%+ membership renewal rate.

FOUNDED ON INTEGRITY
Representing the profession for more than 125 years.

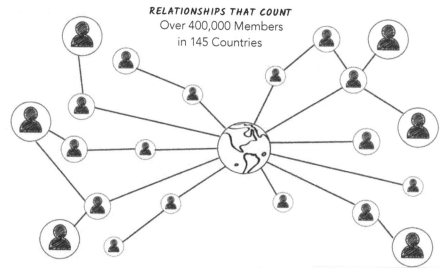

RELATIONSHIPS THAT COUNT
Over 400,000 Members in 145 Countries

TO JOIN, VISIT:
aicpa.org/join or call 888.777.7077.

© 2015 American Institute of CPAs. All rights reserved. 16789-326